A VISUAL GUIDE TO
TECHNOLOGY

Rosen
YA

ALBERTO HERNÁNDEZ PAMPLONA

This edition published in 2018 by
The Rosen Publishing Group, Inc.
29 East 21st Street
New York, NY 10010

Library of Congress Cataloging-in-Publication Data

Names: Pamplona, Alberto Hernández, author.
Title: A visual guide to technology / Alberto Hernández Pamplona.
Description: New York : Rosen Publishing, 2018. | Series: A visual exploration of science | Includes bibliographical references and index. | Audience: Grades 7–12.
Identifiers: LCCN 2017002121 | ISBN 9781508175841 (library-bound)
Subjects: LCSH: Technological innovations—Juvenile literature. | Technology—Juvenile literature.
Classification: LCC T173.8 .P356 2018 | DDC 600—dc23
LC record available at https://lccn.loc.gov/2017002121

Manufactured in the United States of America

Metric Conversion Chart

1 inch = 2.54 centimeters; 25.4 millimeters
1 foot = 30.48 centimeters
1 yard = .914 meters
1 square foot = .093 square meters
1 square mile = 2.59 square kilometers
1 ton = .907 metric tons
1 pound = 454 grams
1 mile = 1.609 kilometers

1 ounce = 28 grams
1 fluid ounce = 30 milliliters
1 teaspoon = 5 milliliters
1 tablespoon = 15 milliliters
1 quart = .946 liters
355 degrees F = 180 degrees Celsius

© 2018 Editorial Sol90, S.L. Barcelona
All Rights Reserved.
Original Edition © 2009 Editorial Sol90, S.L. Barcelona

Original Idea Sol90 Publishing
Project Manegement Nuria Cicero
Editorial Coordination Diana Malizia
Editorial Team Alberto Hernández, Virginia Iris Fernández, Mar Valls, Marta de la Serna, Sebastián Romeu. Maximiliano Ludueña, Carlos Bodyadjan, Doris Elsa Bustamante, Tania Domenicucci, Andrea Giacobone, Constanza Guariglia, Joaquín Hidalgo, Hernán López Winne.
Proofreaders Marta Kordon, Edgardo D'Elio
Design Fabián Cassan
Layout Laura Ocampo, Carolina Berdiñas, Clara Miralles, Paola Fornasaro, Mariana Marx, Pablo Alarcón

Photography Age Fotostock, Getty Images, Science Photo Library, Graphic News, ESA, NASA, National Geographic, Latinstock, Album, ACI, Cordon Press

Infographic Coordination Paula López

Infographies Sol90 Images www.sol90images.com , Paula López, Guillermina Eichel, Pablo Gentile, Maru Hiriart, Maureen Holboll, Clarisa Mateo, Sol Molina, Vanina Ogueta, Gastón Pérsico, Cecilia Szalkowicz, Paula Simonetti

Illustrations Sol90 Images www.sol90images.com , Guido Arroyo, Pablo Aschei, Gustavo J. Caironi, Hernán Cañellas, Leonardo César, José Luis Corsetti, Vanina Farías, Joana Garrido, Celina Hilbert, Isidro López, Diego Martín, Jorge Martínez, Marco Menco, Ala de Mosca, Diego Mourelos, Eduardo Pérez, Javier Pérez, Ariel Piroyansky, Ariel Roldán, Marcel Socías, Néstor Taylor, Trebol Animation, Juan Venegas, Coralia Vignau, 3DN, 3DOM studio, Constanza Vicco, Diego Mourelos.

Contents

NANOROBOT
Microscopic device that is formed by arms scarcely 10 nanometers in length. In the photograph, it is shown transporting a drug through the interior of an infected cell.

Endless Inventiveness

Technologically, humanity today is progressing much quicker than at any point in the past. Nanotechnology, artificial intelligence, and even robots capable of dancing, climbing stairs, and playing chess are no longer confined to the imagination of science-fiction writers—or to the minds of visionary scientists. Nobel Prize in Physics winner Richard Feynman inspired the world in 1959 with a lecture entitled "There's Plenty of Room at the Bottom." He was referring to the universe that exists at the molecular, atomic, and subatomic scales and how its exploitation would revolutionize science and technology. Like Leonardo da Vinci, however, Feynman's ideas were ahead of the tools of his time. When the tools for observing and manipulating atoms began to arrive a few decades later, the fields of medicine, surgery, computing, and especially materials science started to realize Feynman's dream at last. In medicine, for example, researchers have created molecules that can deliver drugs directly to some cancer cells. With a diameter of less than 5 nanometers (millionths of a meter), these nanoparticles can pass through the tiny openings in the cell membranes. It works like a Trojan horse, with a drug enclosed within a nanoparticle coded to resemble some nutrient. Once inside the cancer cell, the nanoparticle releases the drug, killing the diseased cell. There is no doubt that nanotechnology is the science of the new millennium. Nanotechnology is so far-reaching that it will influence all areas of science and technology in ways that are currently unimaginable.

We are still a long way from understanding just how far machines will go. In 50 years, the world will certainly be populated by "smart" robots that will not only be able to play football but will also speak Chinese, English, Japanese, and Korean, as well as autonomously perform tasks such as driving cars and flying planes. These developments are amazing, but they also raise concerns from people who are wary of the prospect of robots that can make unsupervised decisions, particularly if those robots were to be used for military purposes. Remote-controlled robotic soldiers equipped with cameras and machine guns are already in use. The question that some experts are asking is "Who will be to blame if an autonomous robot kills someone?" Caring for the elderly has also raised difficult questions. Robots are already used in Japan to measure basic health indicators, such as blood pressure, in older people. In the future it may be much cheaper to leave the elderly in hospitals to be cared for by machines. Such scenarios make informed debate about robotics very important. For now, the latest surprise comes in the form of Geminoid, the "twin" created by the Japanese professor Hiroshi Ishiguro in his image and likeness—his robotic twin can move around in its chair, blink, and even simulate breathing.

This book presents some of the inventions that have changed the way we perceive the world around us and our daily routines. Here you will discover some of the revolutionary technologies whose appearance truly changed the world. One example is plasma. Who would have imagined that ionized gas, which occurs naturally in the universe, would assume a privileged place in our homes through its use in television screens? Of course, the use of plasma is still in its infancy. According to some experts, the space rockets of the future will be propelled by thin, high-speed plasma jets. Moreover, cold plasma is indispensable for etching the grooves that transmit information on the surface of computer chips. You will also learn about a number of discoveries that have become so fundamental to our daily lives that it is difficult to imagine what the world was like without them, such as the Internet, cellular phones, and digital cameras. Then there are the most recent inventions, which are just starting to reveal their potential. It is surprising to see how many of them are linked in a rich fabric of invention and ingenuity and are applied to further our growth as a species, meeting our needs and shaping our society. ●

Daily-Life Applications

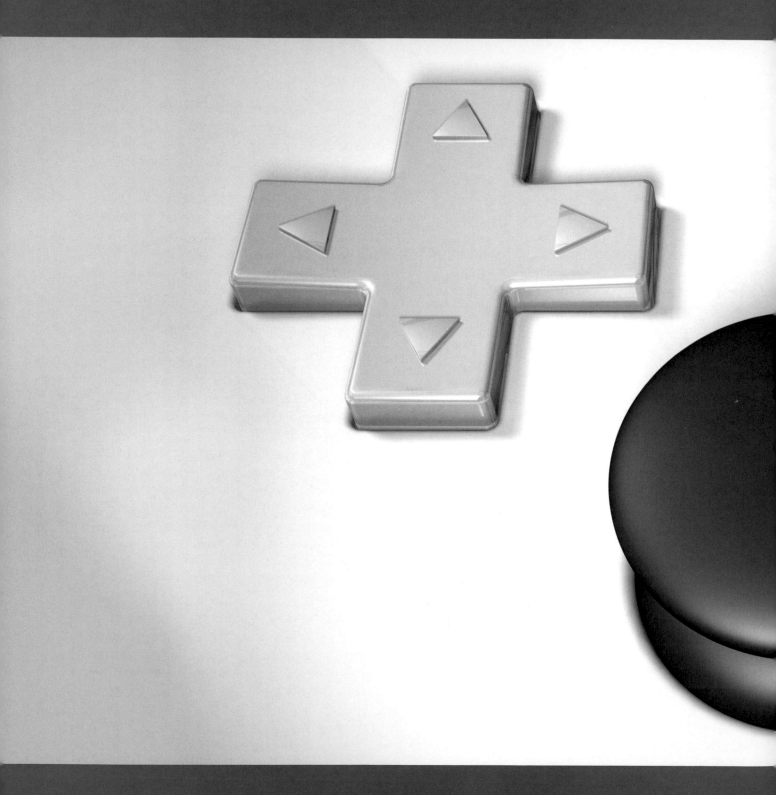

n recent decades, technology has become an integral part of our daily lives, affecting us in a radical and positive way. Liquid crystal displays (LCDs) are found in numerous industrial and consumer devices: vending machines, household appliances, television sets, and computers. The barcode, virtual keyboard, and 3-D printer have transformed the world of

Games Console
With the latest generation of consoles, gamers can connect to monitors, LCD screens, and high-definition TVs to get the most out of their video games.

work and study; the digital camera and video recorder allow us to halt the passage of time, preserving once-in-a-lifetime moments. Our daily lives are shaped by technology. Wherever we look, it offers us what we have always sought: comfort, entertainment, and tools to simplify routine tasks. ●

3-D Movies

The rise of 3-D movie theaters with IMAX technology in the last decade put the public in touch with new ideas in cinematography. The images' high resolution and large size (exceeding human peripheral vision), combined with high-quality sound and three-dimensional effects, attempt to immerse viewers within a movie. At first, only documentary films were shown in these theaters because special filming systems were required. However, in recent years, more and more commercial films have been produced in this format. ●

The Theater

▶ IMAX movie-projection rooms are characterized by their large screen size and their high-quality sound. These two elements, combined with 3-D effects, immerse viewers in the movie.

573 pounds (260 kg) is the average weight of an IMAX film reel. Operators must handle them with cranes.

Projector
has two lenses whose images converge on the screen. Two 15,000-watt lamps are necessary to light such a large screen.

Cooling hoses and pipes

Sound system
Separated into six channels and one subwoofer, for realistic audio

Platters
The two reels display the same movie, from two slightly divergent angles, imitating the human field of vision. They are projected simultaneously.

Filming for IMAX

▶ To achieve 3-D effects, two cameras are used in IMAX filming. Each camera corresponds to a different eye, with the angle of separation reproducing the angle of separation between human eyes.

Because the two cameras cannot be placed close enough to achieve the 3-D effect, a mirror is used to resolve the problem.

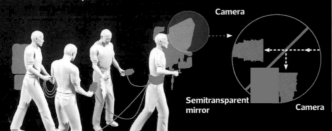

Camera

Semitransparent mirror

Camera

The 3-D Effect

▶ uses two lenses to converge images on the screen. Each lens corresponds to the angle of vision of one of the eyes, and each projection is polarized at an angle perpendicular to the other.

1 Each projector lens polarizes the image at an angle perpendicular to the other.

Horizontal polarization (left eye)

Vertical polarization (right eye)

Comparison with 35-mm Movies

The greatest achievement of IMAX theater in comparison to traditional movie theaters is the size and quality of the images projected, combined with the sound system and 3-D effects.

THE SCREEN
These are the largest screens in the movie industry. They are more than 65 feet (20 m) wide, and the high-resolution projection produces excellent image quality. Because they surpass the normal range of human peripheral vision, viewers feel completely immersed in the film.

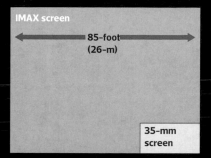

IMAX screen

85-foot (26-m)

35-mm screen

THE FILM
Each frame measures 1.9 by 2.7 inches (50 by 70 mm) and has 15 perforations. In other words, it has 10 times the surface area of the 35-mm film used in traditional projections. Each image corresponds to two frames filmed from slightly different angles, producing a 3-D effect. Unlike conventional movies, the film moves through the projector horizontally—and at much greater speed.

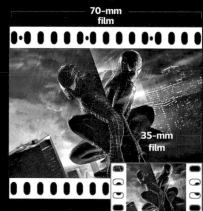

70-mm film

35-mm film

Screen
Of great size and slightly concave

Projection Theaters

IMAX technology allows for two types of theaters: the traditional type with a large, flat screen, and dome-shaped rooms, in which the projection extends to the sides and ceiling.

(2) The eyeglasses used by viewers have perpendicular polarizers corresponding to those of the projector's lenses.

(3) Thus, during the projection of the movie, the polarizers of each eye allow the corresponding image through, blocking the image intended for the other eye.

Traditional
Allows for 3-D effects

Dome
The viewer feels immersed within the film. No 3-D effects.

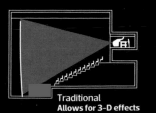

The iPod

This sophisticated multimedia player, introduced by Apple in 2001, once let users store and play up to 80 GB of music, video, and images, encoded in many formats both Mac and PC compatible. Though the iPod has since been replaced by the iPod Touch, introduced in July, 2015, users of any model still download files from iTunes and Apple Music, a newer feature. This software serves as a complex data manager, allowing customers to purchase from a library of more than 26 million songs and numerous videos. ●

Endless Entertainment

One of the most notable features of the attractively designed iPod is its ability to store high-fidelity recordings.

In a size slightly larger than the palm of a person's hand, users can store up to 80 GB of data.

Music
The iPod can store more than 20,000 songs in its 80 GB version (and up to 7,000 songs in its 30 GB version).

Video
The 80 GB version can store and play more than 100 hours of video in various file formats.

Games
The iPod comes with four games, but it is possible to download a large number of games from iTunes.

5 GB iPod

4 inches (10.4 cm)

2.4 inches (6.1 cm)

Images
Stores more than 25,000 images. Plugged into a home theater system, it can display the images with musical accompaniment on a large screen.

Evolution

Since its launch in 2001, the iPod has become smaller, lighter, and more efficient. It now has a color screen, and its maximum storage capacity is 16 times greater than the first model. The iPod spawned a flourishing business in accessories, and it has becom[e a] symbol of an entire generation. Today it is the most popular portable multimedia play[er.]

2001	2004	2004	2005	2005	2005	2007
Original iPod	**Mini iPod**	**U2 iPod**	**iPod Nano**	**iPod Shuffle**	**5G iPod**	**iPod Touch**
The first version of the iPod held 5 GB of information.	Up to 6 GB capacity. Discontinued.	This model was launched in partnership with the band U2 and Universal Music Group.	The successor of the iPod mini. Smaller and lighter, with a color screen. Holds up to 8 GB.	The smallest model, it weighs only 0.5 ounce (15 g) and has no screen.	Holds up to 80 GB; 2.5-inch (6.3-cm) color screen.	A touch screen in full color with access to YouTube

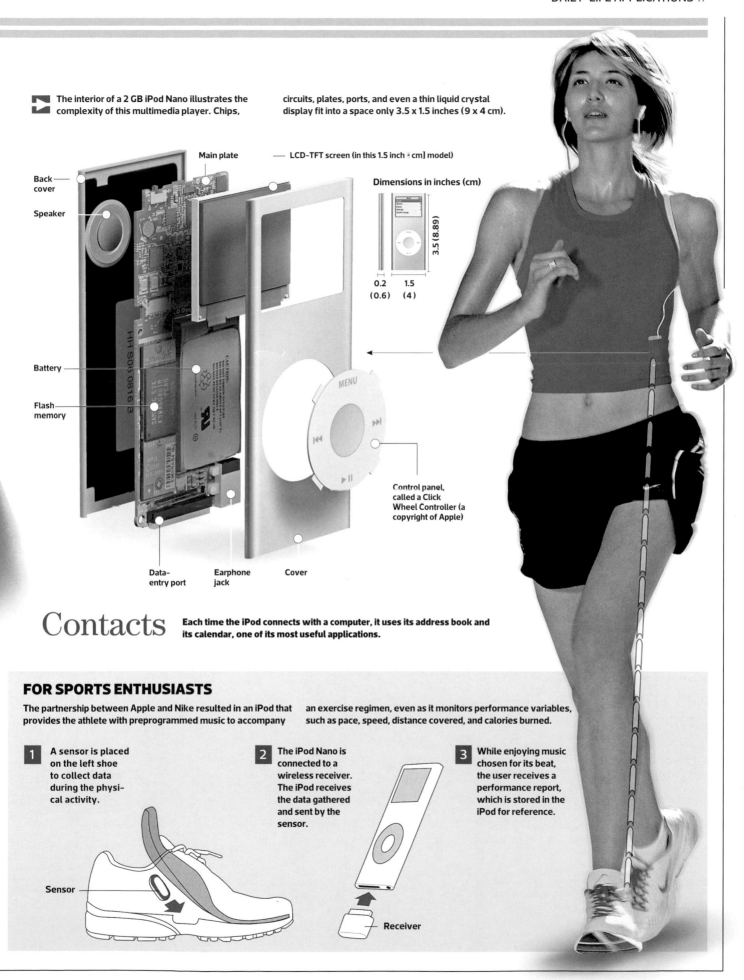

The interior of a 2 GB iPod Nano illustrates the complexity of this multimedia player. Chips, circuits, plates, ports, and even a thin liquid crystal display fit into a space only 3.5 x 1.5 inches (9 x 4 cm).

Main plate

— LCD–TFT screen (in this 1.5 inch ⁴ cm] model)

Back cover

Speaker

Dimensions in inches (cm)

3.5 (8.89)

Battery

Flash memory

0.2 (0.6)   1.5 (4)

MENU

Control panel, called a Click Wheel Controller (a copyright of Apple)

Data-entry port

Earphone jack

Cover

Contacts
Each time the iPod connects with a computer, it uses its address book and its calendar, one of its most useful applications.

FOR SPORTS ENTHUSIASTS

The partnership between Apple and Nike resulted in an iPod that provides the athlete with preprogrammed music to accompany an exercise regimen, even as it monitors performance variables, such as pace, speed, distance covered, and calories burned.

1 A sensor is placed on the left shoe to collect data during the physical activity.

2 The iPod Nano is connected to a wireless receiver. The iPod receives the data gathered and sent by the sensor.

3 While enjoying music chosen for its beat, the user receives a performance report, which is stored in the iPod for reference.

Sensor

Receiver

Nintendo Wii

With the launch of Wii in 2006, Nintendo tried to cause a revolution in the world of video-game consoles. Wii, the fifth generation of Nintendo's video-game consoles and part of the seventh generation of video gaming, succeeded Nintendo's GameCube but was succeeded by the Wii U in 2012, which had a touch-screen interface. Wii has several features intended to help a wider audience play video games and get closer to the world of virtual reality. Among them are sophisticated wireless commands that transfer tactile effects, such as blows and vibrations; infrared sensors that detect the position of the player in a room and convey the information to the console; and separate controls for each hand. ●

Console

The Console

is the brain of Wii. Its slim design (a mere 1.7 inches [4.4 cm] wide) plays the games that are loaded on standard 4.7-inch (12-cm) discs, accepting both single- and double-layered discs.

System

has an IBM PowerPC processor, ports for four controllers, two USB ports, slots for memory expansion, stereo sound, and support for playing videos on panoramic 16:9 screens.

Connectivity

The console connects with the Internet (it includes Wi-Fi wireless connection), from which it can receive updates 24 hours a day to add or upgrade features.

Infrared sensor
detects the player's position from up to a distance of 32 feet (10 m) or 16 feet (5 m) during use of the pointer function (used to indicate points on the screen).

10 meters

250,000

Wii consoles were manufactured daily by Nintendo. In preparation for the Wii's launch in Japan, 400,000 units were manufactured (an unprecedented quantity for a new console), all of which were sold within a few hours.

Vibrator
generates vibrations appropriate for the situation, such as when shooting a gun or hitting a ball.

Internal speaker
reproduces sounds, such as gunshots or the clash of swords.

Console buttons
(holding down both buttons activates Wiimote's discovery mode, which can be used to set it up to work with a Bluetooth-enabled PC)

LED light
indicates which player is active in multiplayer games.

The Wiimote

The Wiimote, the Wii's remote, differs from traditional game consoles by looking more like a remote control than a videogame controller. It was developed to be useable with just one hand.

The Movement Sensor

A player's movements are detected by means of a flexible silicon bar inside the Wiimote. This bar moves within an electric field generated by capacitors. The player's movements cause the bar to change the electric field. The change is detected and transmitted to the infrared sensor, which translates it into the movements of the virtual character.

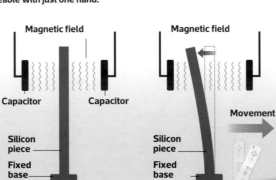

Magnetic field

Capacitor | Capacitor

Silicon piece

Fixed base

Magnetic field

Silicon piece

Fixed base

Movement

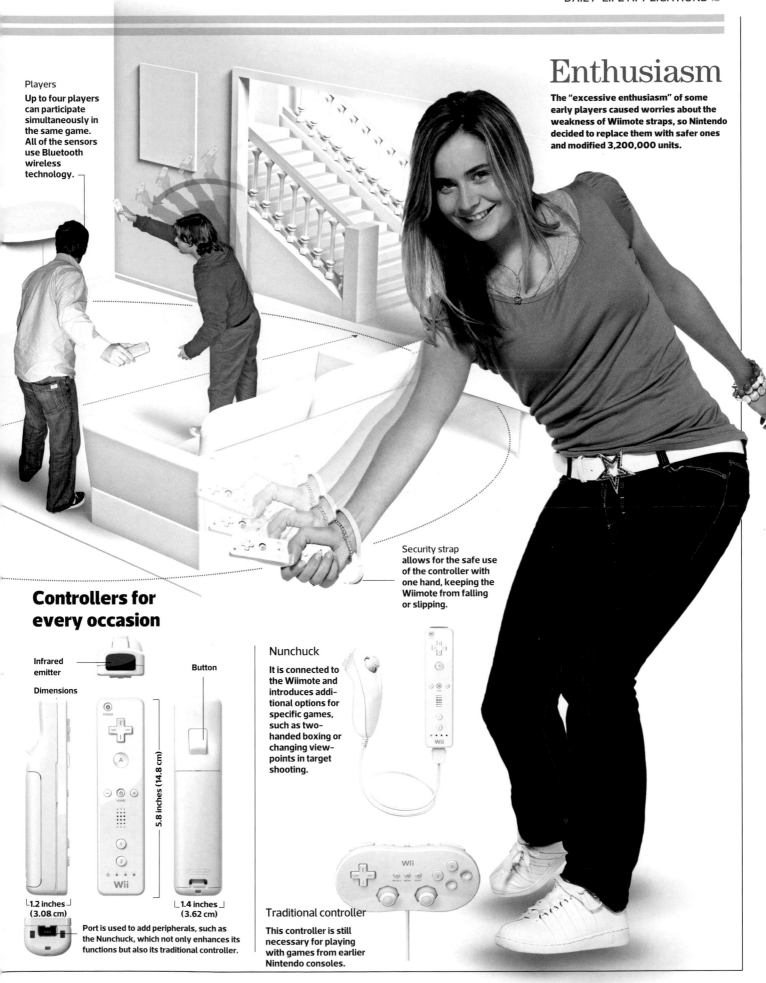

Players

Up to four players can participate simultaneously in the same game. All of the sensors use Bluetooth wireless technology.

Enthusiasm

The "excessive enthusiasm" of some early players caused worries about the weakness of Wiimote straps, so Nintendo decided to replace them with safer ones and modified 3,200,000 units.

Security strap
allows for the safe use of the controller with one hand, keeping the Wiimote from falling or slipping.

Controllers for every occasion

Infrared emitter

Button

Dimensions

5.8 inches (14.8 cm)

POWER

A

HOME

1

2

Wii

1.2 inches (3.08 cm)

1.4 inches (3.62 cm)

Port is used to add peripherals, such as the Nunchuck, which not only enhances its functions but also its traditional controller.

Nunchuck

It is connected to the Wiimote and introduces additional options for specific games, such as two-handed boxing or changing view-points in target shooting.

Wii

Traditional controller

This controller is still necessary for playing with games from earlier Nintendo consoles.

LCDs

The technology used in the displays of small cell phones and laptops is based on the use of liquid crystals—a discovery dating back to the 19th century. This technology has been applied to television sets, causing a revolution in terms of size and image quality. LCD televisions are flatter and lighter than conventional sets and need less power to operate. ●

INSIDE THE SCREEN

LED BULBS

State-of-the-art screens use diodes, which emit red, green, and blue light. Together these colors form a powerful white light that replaces traditional fluorescent tubes.

DIFFUSER

controls brightness and softens the light.

CIRCUITS

convert the TV signal into electric instructions for the liquid crystal to use in forming the image on the screen.

LIQUID CRYSTAL

Discovered at the end of the 19th century, liquid crystals share characteristics of both solids and liquids. Their molecules can have a specific crystalline structure—which is characteristic of solids—but still have some freedom of movement. In LCDs, crystals can be oriented by electric impulses while staying in place.

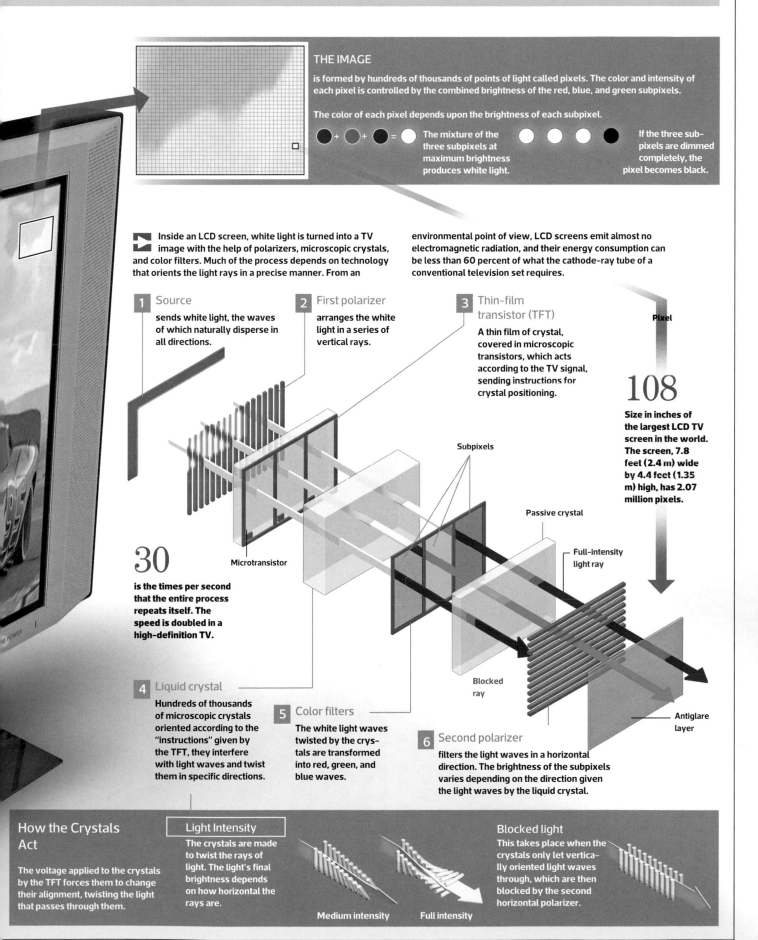

THE IMAGE

is formed by hundreds of thousands of points of light called pixels. The color and intensity of each pixel is controlled by the combined brightness of the red, blue, and green subpixels.

The color of each pixel depends upon the brightness of each subpixel.

● + ● + ● = ○ The mixture of the three subpixels at maximum brightness produces white light.

○ ○ ○ ● If the three subpixels are dimmed completely, the pixel becomes black.

Inside an LCD screen, white light is turned into a TV image with the help of polarizers, microscopic crystals, and color filters. Much of the process depends on technology that orients the light rays in a precise manner. From an environmental point of view, LCD screens emit almost no electromagnetic radiation, and their energy consumption can be less than 60 percent of what the cathode-ray tube of a conventional television set requires.

1 Source

sends white light, the waves of which naturally disperse in all directions.

2 First polarizer

arranges the white light in a series of vertical rays.

3 Thin-film transistor (TFT)

A thin film of crystal, covered in microscopic transistors, which acts according to the TV signal, sending instructions for crystal positioning.

Pixel

108

Size in inches of the largest LCD TV screen in the world. The screen, 7.8 feet (2.4 m) wide by 4.4 feet (1.35 m) high, has 2.07 million pixels.

Subpixels

Passive crystal

Full-intensity light ray

30

is the times per second that the entire process repeats itself. The speed is doubled in a high-definition TV.

Microtransistor

Blocked ray

4 Liquid crystal

Hundreds of thousands of microscopic crystals oriented according to the "instructions" given by the TFT, they interfere with light waves and twist them in specific directions.

5 Color filters

The white light waves twisted by the crystals are transformed into red, green, and blue waves.

6 Second polarizer

filters the light waves in a horizontal direction. The brightness of the subpixels varies depending on the direction given the light waves by the liquid crystal.

Antiglare layer

How the Crystals Act

The voltage applied to the crystals by the TFT forces them to change their alignment, twisting the light that passes through them.

Light Intensity

The crystals are made to twist the rays of light. The light's final brightness depends on how horizontal the rays are.

Medium intensity　　Full intensity

Blocked light

This takes place when the crystals only let vertically oriented light waves through, which are then blocked by the second horizontal polarizer.

Digital TV

The arrival of plasma and liquid crystal (LCD) televisions has taken picture quality to unprecedented levels. However, the revolution would not have been complete without the explosive development of digital TV, which has nearly replaced traditional analog TV completely throughout most of the world in the past decade. The concept involves the digitization of the entire process, from the capturing of the images to the arrival in homes of something that enables users to interact with digital TV channels and culminates in high-definition digital TV (HDTV), which offers the best televised picture quality available with current technology. ●

A World of "Ones" and "Zeros"

The digital TV process begins in the actual TV studio, continues with consoles and storage methods via transmission systems, and ends with the broadcast on each television set.

1 Image
High-resolution digital cameras capture images and encode the data as "ones" and "zeros."

2 Storage
Information is transmitted to consoles, which work with online servers and digital storage methods via high-speed systems.

3 Transmission
The transmission process uses compressed digital formats, which make it possible to send massive flows of information at very high speeds via either cable or satellite.

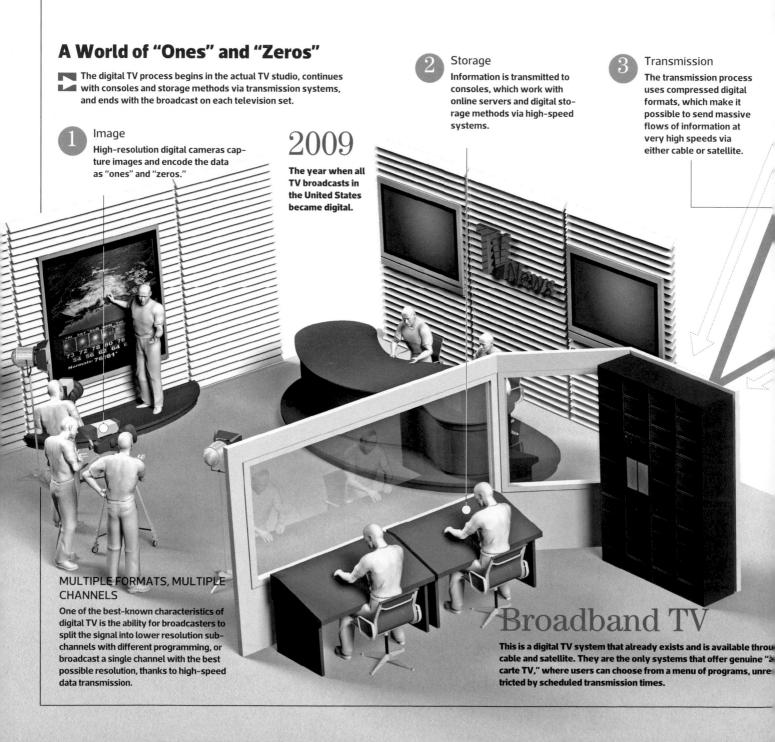

2009
The year when all TV broadcasts in the United States became digital.

MULTIPLE FORMATS, MULTIPLE CHANNELS

One of the best-known characteristics of digital TV is the ability for broadcasters to split the signal into lower resolution subchannels with different programming, or broadcast a single channel with the best possible resolution, thanks to high-speed data transmission.

Broadband TV

This is a digital TV system that already exists and is available throu[gh] cable and satellite. They are the only systems that offer genuine "à [la] carte TV," where users can choose from a menu of programs, unre[s]tricted by scheduled transmission times.

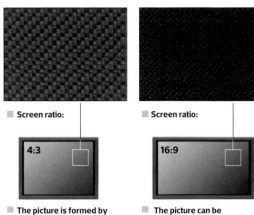

Picture Quality

The concept of digital TV is that "viewers see either the best quality images, or nothing." The system eliminates ghosts, distortion, and color errors. Optimum picture quality is determined by two factors: the proportions of the image and the resolution.

30% larger

A 16:9 screen is 30% larger than a 4:3 screen, for the same horizontal resolution (lines of pixels).

ANALOG TV

- Screen ratio: **4:3**
- The picture is formed by up to 211,000 pixels.

DIGITAL TV

- Screen ratio: **16:9**
- The picture can be formed by more than 2 million pixels.

A LA CARTE

Depending on the service, users can choose between different programming options, consult guides, and pay to view programs.

5 Interactivity

Unlike analog TV, in digital transmissions input and output paths are established, giving the user a degree of interactivity with the broadcaster.

4 Decompression

The information is decompressed and processed by a decoder before being interpreted and converted into TV images.

CABLE DISTRIBULATORS

SOUND

The sound is received in Dolby Digital 5.1., that Is, on five channels separated by the relative position of each one, which creates a three-dimensional effect if a home theater system is used.

DECODER

With digital TV, the TV set performs a similar function to that of a TV monitor. Traditional analog TV, however, is set up to receive the signals from different broadcasters directly.

Different Formats

	Analog	SDTV	EDTV	HDTV	HDTV
Pixels	211,000	307,200	337,920	921,600	2,073,600
Resolution	640 x 480	640 x 480	704 x 480	1,280 x 720	1,920 x 1,080
Scanning Format	480 lines	480 lines	480 pixels	720 pixels	1,080 lines
Screen	4:3	4:3	4:3 or 16:9	16:9	16:9
Quality	Average	Good	Very good	Excellent	Excellent

Interlaced Scanning

This is the method used in traditional color TV transmissions. The screen is divided into horizontal lines of pixels. The odd and even lines are each refreshed 60 times a second, at alternating intervals. The complete picture, therefore, is updated 30 times a second.

Progressive Scanning

The entire picture is refreshed 60 times a second, giving exceptional picture quality. In high-definition digital TV, there are two equivalent formats. With 720p, progressive scanning is used, but for 720 lines of pixels. With 1080i, there are more lines of pixels, but the scanning is interlaced. Still higher resolution is given by 1080p broadcasts.

Virtual Laser Keyboard

G iven that a simple wireless keyboard still surprises some people, a virtual laser keyboard might seem like a fantastic invention from a science-fiction movie. Yet it is already a reality and can be bought at an affordable price, unlike other alternative keyboards. Users "write" on a virtual keyboard that can be projected onto a wide variety of surfaces. Far from being a technological fad or a gimmick with no real use, the virtual laser keyboard is the answer to a serious problem: writing on applications that use PDA technology is often very difficult because of the small size of the keys. ●

Writing in Light

▶ A tiny device, smaller than a cellular phone, is all that is needed to generate the virtual keyboard, which can be projected onto any opaque surface.

PDA Device
An electronic organizer, Palm Pilot, cellular phone, or other device receives the typed information via a Bluetooth connection, displaying the information on its screen.

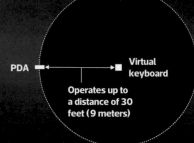

PDA ◄──────■ Virtual keyboard

Operates up to a distance of 30 feet (9 meters)

400

The minimum number of characters per minute that the virtual keyboard can interpret, which means a professional typist can enter around 80 words per minute.

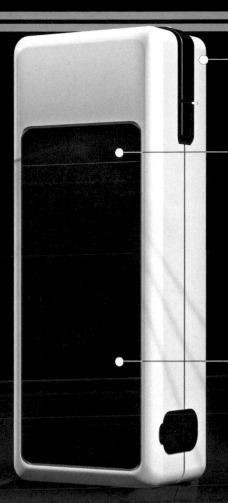

Projector

This is the heart of the virtual keyboard. It measures just 3.6 inches (9.2 cm) x 1.4 inches (3.5 cm) and weighs 3 ounces (90 grams).

Projection window

Projection surface

Virtual keyboard

It is a laser projection, equivalent to a small keyboard: 11.5 inches (29.5 cm) x 3.75 inches (9.5 cm).

How Does It Work?

Although the user writes on the virtual laser keyboard, detection is actually performed with the help of an invisible infrared layer, located directly above the virtual keyboard.

1 The laser projector generates the virtual keyboard onto an opaque surface. At the same time, a diode generates an infrared layer, parallel to the keyboard, located less than 0.12 inch above the projection.

— Virtual keyboard
— Infrared layer

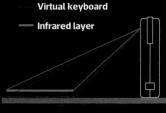

2 When the user presses one of the projected keys, the infrared light field is broken, producing an ultraviolet reflection, which is also invisible.

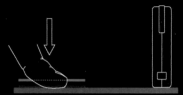

3 The reflection is picked up by a camera, which sends the signal to a chip. This chip calculates the position of the key that has been "pressed," based on the distance and angle of reflection.

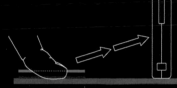

4 The information is transmitted via an infrared Bluetooth connection to the PDA, which displays the selected character on its screen.

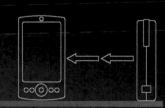

15 minutes

The practice time needed to get the hang of the virtual keyboard, according to the manufacturer

Other Alternative Keyboards

Ergonomic Keyboards

There are numerous, strangely shaped models. However, they all promise to make typing more comfortable and, in many cases, less painful.

OrbiTouch Keyless Keyboard

Without a doubt, this is one of the most unusual keyboards out there. In fact, it has no keys at all, just two domes that, using wrist movements, allow the user to write 128 characters and use 3 mouse combinations.

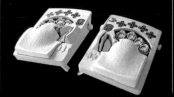

DataHand Ergonomic Keyboard

This device fits perfectly into the palm of the hand and even has a built-in mouse. The idea is to reduce the stress caused to fingers by long days of typing. The user selects the keys that appear on the key assignment display.

Roll-Up Keyboard

This is similar to a standard keyboard in every way, except one: it is flexible and can even be rolled up.

Memory Stick

Although it has been almost three decades since the USB (Universal Serial Bus) flash drive appeared in stores, this small storage device, which uses flash memory to save information without the need for batteries, remains among the physical choices for data storage and transportation. It is small, durable, lightweight, quick, reliable, and very practical, and it has proven extremely versatile for more complex uses, such as the ability to start up any computer using specific stored parameters. Its capabilities are increasing all the time, and today it is cheaper and easier to buy devices that can store many gigabytes (billions of bytes). ●

Flash Memory: The Key

Flash memory has several characteristics that have revolutionized the storage capacity of small devices such as cameras and cellular phones: it is nonvolatile, meaning that the memory is not erased when the power is off; and it is a semiconductor rather than some type of spinning magnetic or optical disk, making it faster and physically more robust.

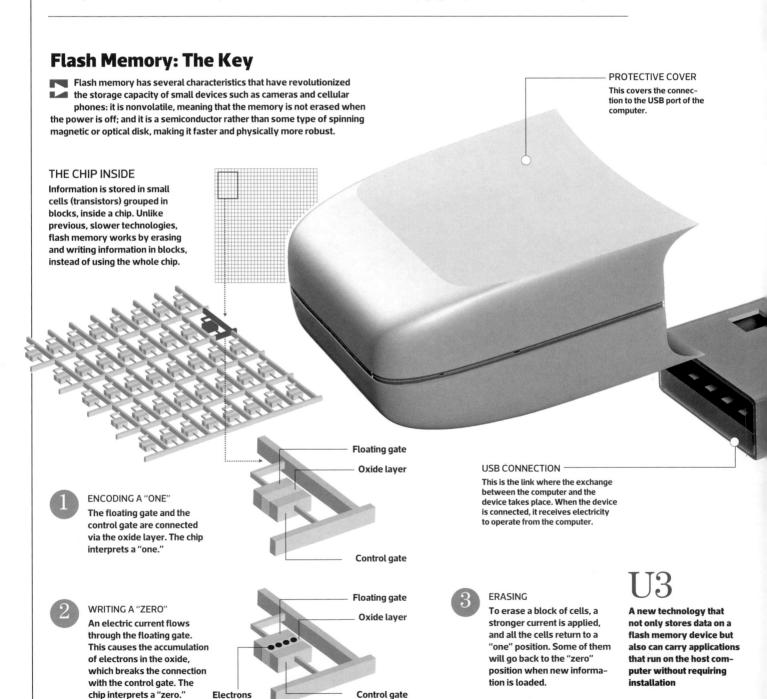

PROTECTIVE COVER
This covers the connection to the USB port of the computer.

THE CHIP INSIDE
Information is stored in small cells (transistors) grouped in blocks, inside a chip. Unlike previous, slower technologies, flash memory works by erasing and writing information in blocks, instead of using the whole chip.

1 ENCODING A "ONE"
The floating gate and the control gate are connected via the oxide layer. The chip interprets a "one."

Floating gate
Oxide layer
Control gate

2 WRITING A "ZERO"
An electric current flows through the floating gate. This causes the accumulation of electrons in the oxide, which breaks the connection with the control gate. The chip interprets a "zero."

Floating gate
Oxide layer
Electrons
Control gate

USB CONNECTION
This is the link where the exchange between the computer and the device takes place. When the device is connected, it receives electricity to operate from the computer.

3 ERASING
To erase a block of cells, a stronger current is applied, and all the cells return to a "one" position. Some of them will go back to the "zero" position when new information is loaded.

U3

A new technology that not only stores data on a flash memory device but also can carry applications that run on the host computer without requiring installation

10 years

In theory, this is the useful life of a USB flash drive device. Taking into account the speed of technological advances, it is likely that the majority of these devices will cease to be used before then, as they will become obsolete.

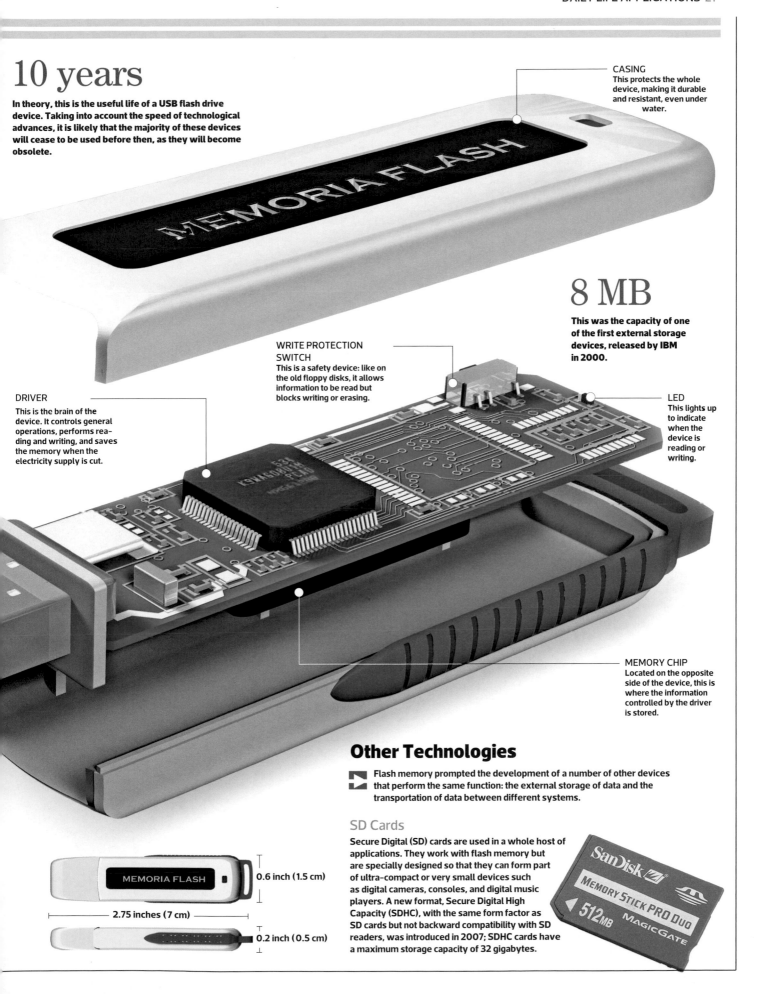

CASING
This protects the whole device, making it durable and resistant, even under water.

8 MB

This was the capacity of one of the first external storage devices, released by **IBM** in 2000.

WRITE PROTECTION SWITCH
This is a safety device: like on the old floppy disks, it allows information to be read but blocks writing or erasing.

DRIVER
This is the brain of the device. It controls general operations, performs reading and writing, and saves the memory when the electricity supply is cut.

LED
This lights up to indicate when the device is reading or writing.

MEMORY CHIP
Located on the opposite side of the device, this is where the information controlled by the driver is stored.

MEMORIA FLASH

0.6 inch (1.5 cm)

2.75 inches (7 cm)

0.2 inch (0.5 cm)

Other Technologies

Flash memory prompted the development of a number of other devices that perform the same function: the external storage of data and the transportation of data between different systems.

SD Cards

Secure Digital (SD) cards are used in a whole host of applications. They work with flash memory but are specially designed so that they can form part of ultra-compact or very small devices such as digital cameras, consoles, and digital music players. A new format, Secure Digital High Capacity (SDHC), with the same form factor as SD cards but not backward compatibility with SD readers, was introduced in 2007; SDHC cards have a maximum storage capacity of 32 gigabytes.

SanDisk
MEMORY STICK PRO DUO
512MB
MAGICGATE

The Digital Camera

T he word "photography" comes from Greek words which, combined, mean "to draw with light" (from *photos*, or "light," and *graphis*, or "drawing"). Photography is the technique of recording fixed images on a light–sensitive surface. Digital cameras are based on the principles of traditional photography, but, instead of fixing images on film coated with chemical substances sensitive to light, they process the intensity of the light and store the data in digital files. Modern digital cameras generally have multiple functions and are able to record sound and video in addition to photographs. ●

The Digital System

1 IMAGE CAPTURE

Digital image
The image appears upside down and laterally inverted.

Object

Objective
The objective focuses the image, refracting the light rays that arrive from the object so that they converge into a coherent image.

Diaphragm
It determines the amount of light that enters through the lens. This is measured in f–numbers. The greater the f–number, the smaller the opening of the diaphragm.

Shutter
The shutter determines the length of the exposure. It is generally measured in fractions of a second. The faster the shutter, the shorter the exposure.

CCD

THE SENSOR THAT REPLACES FILM

The CCD (charge-coupled device) is a group of small diodes sensitive to light (photosites), which convert photons (light) into electrons (electric charges).

CCD

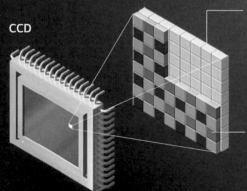

Photosites
are light-sensitive cells. The amount of light shining on the photosites is directly proportional to the electric charge that is accumulated.

Filters
To generate a color image, a series of filters must unpack the image into discrete values of red, green, and blue (RGB).

A Long Evolution

The camera obscura
Light rays reflected by an object pass through a tiny hole and are projected as an inverted image within a box. A lens concentrates the light and focuses the image. Mirrors are used to reflect the image on a flat surface, and an artist traces the projected image.

1500

A light-sensitive substance
Experiments by the German scientist Frederick Schulze prove that light blackens silver nitrate.

1725

The optical and chemical principles are combined.
Images are created by placing sheets directly over the light-sensitive paper and exposing them to sunlight. The images cannot be fixed.

1802

Nicéphore Niépce
exposes a tin plate, covered with bitumen, to light for eight hours. The bitumen hardens and turns white from the exposure, producing an image. The non-hardened areas are then washed away.

1826

The daguerreotype
The daguerreotype obtained finely detailed images on copper plates covered with silver and photosensitized with iodine. The images (single and positive) are developed with mercury vapor and fixed with saline solution.

1839

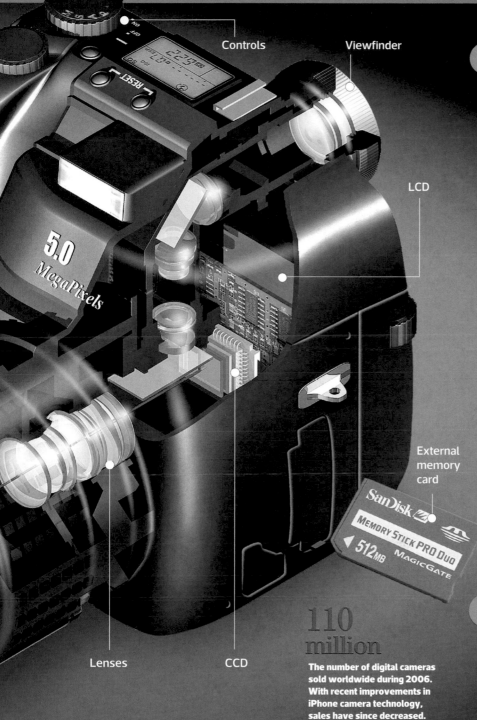

Controls

Viewfinder

LCD

5.0 MegaPixels

External memory card

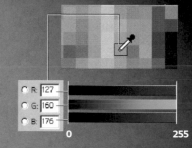

SanDisk
MEMORY STICK PRO DUO
512MB MAGICGATE

Lenses

CCD

Binary system processing

To convert the electric charges of the photosite (analog) to digital signals, the camera uses a converter (ADC), which assigns a binary value to each one of the charges stored in the photosite, storing them as pixels (points of color).

ADDITIVE MIXTURE

Each pixel is colored by mixing values of RGB. Varying quantities of each of these colors can reproduce almost any color of the visible spectrum.

R: 127
G: 160
B: 176

0   255

The value of each can vary from 0 (darkness) to 255 (the greatest color intensity).

RESOLUTION

is measured in PPIs, or pixels per square inch—the number of pixels that can be captured by a digital camera. This figure indicates the size and quality of the image.

Compression and storage

Once the image is digitized, a microprocessor compresses the data in memory as JPG or TIFF files.

110 million

The number of digital cameras sold worldwide during 2006. With recent improvements in iPhone camera technology, sales have since decreased.

The calotype

Invented by Talbot, this is the first positive-to-negative process. The exposures last from one to five minutes. An unlimited number of prints could be reproduced from a single negative.

1841

Glass plates

The substitution of paper for a glass plate is perfected. The plates are sensitized with silver nitrate, which received the negative image. The exposure is only a few seconds.

1851

In color

The Scottish physicist James Clerk Maxwell obtains the first color photograph by using light filters to produce three separate negatives.

1861

Flexible film

The Kodak camera uses a roll of photosensitized celluloid film. The film could be used for 100 photographs using exposures of only a fraction of a second.

1889

Color photograph

The Lumière brothers perfect the procedure of using glass plates covered with different colored grains to produce images formed by tiny points of primary colors.

1907

The video photograph

Sony produces a reflex camera that records images on a magnetic disc. The images could be viewed on a television set.

1989

GPS

he Global Positioning System (GPS) allows people to locate their position nearly anywhere on the planet, at any time, using a small handheld receiver. Originally developed as a military project, GPS has now reached every corner of civilian life. Today it is not only an essential tool in ships and aircraft but has also become, due to its multiple applications, a common feature in vehicles as well as athletic and scientific equipment. ●

Features

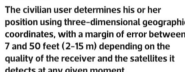 Since GPS is a dynamic system, it also provides real-time data about the movement, direction, and speed of the user, allowing for a myriad of uses.

1 Location
The civilian user determines his or her position using three-dimensional geographic coordinates, with a margin of error between 7 and 50 feet (2-15 m) depending on the quality of the receiver and the satellites it detects at any given moment.

2 Maps
Extrapolation of the coordinates using geographic charts of cities, roads, rivers, oceans, and airspace can produce a dynamic map of the user's position and movement.

3 Tracking
The user can know the speed at which he or she is traveling, the distance traveled, and the time elapsed. In addition, other information is provided, such as average speed.

4 Trips
Trips can be programmed using predetermined points (waypoints). During the trip, the GPS receiver provides information about the remaining distance to each waypoint, the correct direction, and the estimated time of arrival.

I-80

EXIT N RT-15 / JEFFERSON /

4.4 mi | 01:30 | 70 mi

Icon and name of the next waypoint (in this case, an exit)

Distance to the next waypoint

Time elapsed

Direction to the next waypoint

Speed

APPLICATIONS

Although it was originally developed as a navigational system, GPS is used today in a variety of fields. The free use of this tool for work, business, recreation, and sports activities is changing the way we move and act.

SPORTS
GPS devices keep the athlete informed on time, speed, and distance.

MILITARY
Used in remote-controlled and navigational systems

SCIENTIFIC
Used in paleontology, archaeology, and animal tracking

EXPLORATION
Provides orientation and marks reference points

TRANSPORTATION
Air and maritime navigation. Its use is growing in automobiles.

AGRICULTURE
Maps areas of greater or lesser fertility within different plots of land

Satellites, Lighthouses in the Sky

The Navstar GPS satellites are the heart of the system. The satellites emit signals that are interpreted by the GPS receiver to determine its location on a map. The system has a constellation of 24 main satellites that orbit the Earth at an altitude of 12,550 miles (20,200 km), collectively covering the entire surface of the planet. They circle the Earth every 12 hours.

1 The receiver detects one of the satellites and calculates its distance. This distance is the radius of a sphere whose center is the satellite and on whose surface the user can be located, although at a point yet to be determined.

2 When a second satellite is detected and the distance calculated, a second sphere is formed that intersects with the first sphere along a circle. The user can be located anywhere along the perimeter of this circle.

3 A third satellite forms a third sphere that intersects the circle at two points. One of the points is ruled out as an invalid location (for example, a position above the surface of the Earth). The other point is the correct location. The more satellites used, the lower the margin of error.

Clocks

Thanks to data received from the satellites, civilian GPS receivers also function as atomic clocks (the most precise in the world), although several thousands of dollars cheaper.

CALCULATING DISTANCES

Once the GPS satellites are detected by the GPS receiver, the receiver's challenge is to precisely calculate its distance and position in relation to those satellites.

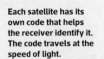

1 The receiver has in its memory the satellites' ephemerides (from the Greek word *ephemeros*, meaning "daily")—that is, their position in the sky by the hour and day.

2 Upon detection of a satellite, it receives a highly complex signal of on-off pulses called a pseudo-random code.

Each satellite has its own code that helps the receiver identify it. The code travels at the speed of light.

Satellite code

Satellite code

Receiver code

3 The receiver recognizes the code and the exact time of each repetition (the signal includes corrections to the receiver's clock). By means of comparison, the receiver determines the lag in the satellite's signal, and since it knows the signal's speed, it can determine the distance.

Lag

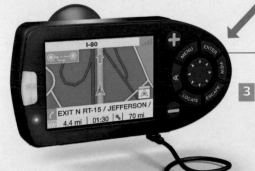
I-80
EXIT N RT-15 / JEFFERSON /
4.4 mi   01:30   70 mi

750 The annual cost, in millions of dollars, to maintain the entire Global Positioning System.

E-paper

ntil a few years ago, the idea of electronic screens as thin as a sheet of paper and so flexible they could be rolled up and folded might have seemed incredible. This technology can now be found in some electronic books and as a means of adding functionality to watches and mobile phones. Additional benefits of e-paper screens include excellent visibility from any angle and in any environment, even in direct sunlight, and extremely low-energy consumption.

Paper-thin

The main advantage of e-paper screens is their thinness and flexibility. Screens 0.05-inch (1.2-mm) thick are already on the market.

2.19 inches (5.56 cm)

4 inches (10 cm)

Book: The Hitchhikers Guide
st read: Today, 14:15

5S Feeds
est: Polymer Vision show

odcasts
est: CNN world up

nail
est: Meeting

rsonal i
enda,

radius

0.012 inch (0.3 mm)

The thickness of a prototype electronic paper screen presented by E Ink Corporation. That is equivalent to half the thickness of a credit card.

Headphone socket

USB port
Enables connection to a PC, modem, printer, or any other hardware

Polymer Vision

Spherical Secret

➡ E-paper technology is based on the use of thousands of spheres located between a pair of electrodes. Each sphere is filled with small positively and negatively charged black-and-white particles that respond to electric stimuli and jointly form an image.

When the lower electrode is positively charged, the white particles rise, forming a white dot on the image.

When the lower electrode is negatively charged, the black particles rise, forming a black dot on the screen.

When the charge in the lower electrode is mixed, both black and white particles rise. This makes it possible to obtain smaller black and white pixels and therefore to achieve an image resolution of up to 150 dots per inch.

Upper electrode
(transparent)

+

+

−

Lower
electrode

+

−

Challenges

The greatest challenges for e-paper technology are to develop an efficient color screen (prototypes have already been made) and to improve the refresh rate so that it will be possible to display videos smoothly.

Screen
Currently available in 5, 6, 8, and 9.7 inches (13, 15, 20, and 25 cm), although there are prototypes measuring up to 40 inches (100 cm).

Applications

➡ The applications are infinite and range from billboards to as far as the imagination can stretch. Here are some of the most viable applications in the short term.

Electronic Newspapers and Books

This is one of the most promising areas. It has the flexibility of normal paper plus all the applications of an electronic screen.

Watches

As well as having great optical qualities, e-paper will open up design possibilities because of the flexibility of the screen.

Cellular Phones

For monochrome displays with enhanced image quality, even in direct sunlight

3-D Printers

The launch of 3-D printers brought an inexpensive and practical alternative to large industrial modeling machines. Of similar size to—or even smaller than—a photocopier, they can quickly and easily create three-dimensional objects, especially models, in a wide range of formats, from very simple to highly complex, and recently even in color. They are controlled by a normal computer using special 3-D modeling software and are very efficient because they have the option to reuse waste materials. ●

The Printer

can build 3-D objects from 8 to 12 inches (20-30 cm) in length, depending on the model, using a special powder of fine particles and an adhesive material that acts like glue.

The leftover powder is stored and reused.

Mobile frame
The frame moves from left to right covering the whole work area, allowing the print head to move over the object being built.

Adhesive tube
Carries the adhesive material to the print head

Print head
Moves around the axis of the frame perpendicularly, injecting the adhesive ink onto the powder, according to the instructions from the processor

Powder tray
Stores the powder used to build the object. During printing, the tray rises slowly to ensure a continuous supply of powder.

Modeling tray
Collects the powder, layer by layer, while the print head models the object with the adhesive ink. During printing, it moves downward. On completion, it will contain the finished object.

0.004 inch (0.1 mm)

is the average thickness of each layer in the construction of a 3-D object.

Computerized Sculpting

3-D printing builds objects layer by layer, from the base to the top. It is a slow process, but it is quicker and cheaper than building models in the traditional way.

1 The Design
Created on a computer screen, using a 3-D modeling program

2 The Base
The print head sprays a fine layer of powder into the modeling tray.

Powder tray

Powder

Powder tray

Modeling tray

3 The Print Process
The quick-drying adhesive ink is then injected onto the layer of powder. This process is repeated for each layer of the object.

Powder tray

Modelling tray

4 Finishing Stages
Once completed, the object is removed from the modeling tray. Finally, it is dipped in various liquids to achieve the desired rigidity.

A Printer at Home

Because of the high cost of 3-D printers, they are usually found only in large organizations. However, the Fab@home Project aims to enable users to build their own printers at a very low cost and use them to produce 3-D objects in various materials such as plastics, chocolate, and cheese.

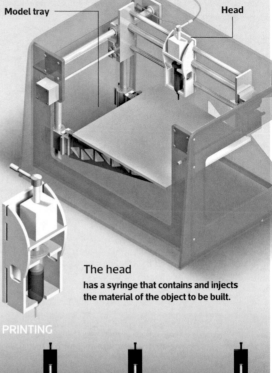

Model tray

Head

The head
has a syringe that contains and injects the material of the object to be built.

PRINTING

Does not require a 3-D substratum such as powder. The head builds the object layer by layer on the mobile platform. It tends to be a very slow but economical process.

In Color

The new models of 3-D printers incorporate four adhesive ink heads—cyan, yellow, magenta, and black—which make it possible to create 3-D objects of any color.

Barcode

t is unlikely that the globalized mass market could operate at its current level without the barcode, a two-color label that encodes information about a given product and, using an optical scanner, enables that product to be identified within a fraction of a second. Although the barcode frequently crops up in daily life, particularly in supermarkets, it has a wide range of applications, especially in the logistics, transportation, and distribution of goods. Barcodes are even used on mobile devices as Quick Response (QR) codes. ●

Speed Reading

▶ The necessary companion to the barcode is the optical reader or scanner, which, in less than a second, can "read" the product information contained in the code.

1 The product is placed as perpendicularly as possible in front of the reader so that the bar-code is lit up by the beam of the laser.

2 The red laser emitted by the reader scans the code. The black bars absorb the red light, whe-reas the white bars reflect it.

3 The reflections are picked up by a reading device, which sends a signal to a decoder. The decoder converts the bars into a binary numeric code and then into a decimal code.

4 The processor compares the numeric code with those in its database and thus identifies the product. When it identifies the product, the processor obtains other information, which is not included in the barcode, such as its price and name.

Applications

▶ The best-known application of the barcode is the scanning of goods at supermarket checkouts. However, it has many other uses:

- Quality Control

- Production Control

- Tracking Packages

- Shipping and Receiving

- Orders and Restocking

2
LASER

Error Rate

On average, the barcode generates 1 error per 100,000 readings.

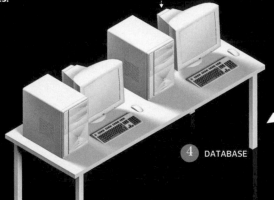

CHECKOUT

4 DATABASE

1972

The year the barcode was used for the first time at a supermarket checkout. It was at a branch of the Kroger chain, in Cincinnati, Ohio.

The Code

A 13-digit number is encoded using a series of bars and spaces of varying widths. This number contains three types of data: the origin of the product, the company that produced it, and specific information about the product. There is also a check digit.

Bars and spaces

The red laser emitted by the reader scans the code. The black bars absorb the red light, whereas the white bars reflect it.

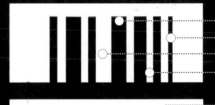

Láser

0 121200 97815 9

CHECK DIGIT
A mathematical formula is obtained from the 12 previous digits. This enables the system to detect incidents of fraud or transmission and reading errors.

DIGITS IDENTIFYING THE ORIGIN

DIGITS IDENTIFYING THE PRODUCING COMPANY

DIGITS IDENTIFYING THE ITEM

Symbology

Each of the 13 digits that form the number is encoded using the binary system, with ones and zeros. The ones and zeros are defined by the width of the bars and spaces.

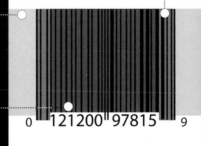

Wide bar: 1
Narrow bar: 1
Wide space: 0
Narrow space: 0

Quiet zone

This is an empty space that enables the reader to distinguish the code from the rest of the product label.

Start and end bars

These bars do not encode numbers. They simply indicate the start and end of the code.

Coding zone

Contains information about the origin, the company, and the product itself

0 121200 97815 9

READING DEVICE

MIRRORS

Colors and Contrasts

The bars and spaces must contrast so that the scanner can read the barcode. However, a number of color combinations can be used in addition to black and white.

Combinations That Work

Black and White	Blue and White	Green and White	Black and Yellow	Black and Orange	Black and Red

Combinations That Do Not Work

Yellow and White	Red and White	Black and Green	Black and Brown	Red and Gold	Blue and Green

Other Codes

EAN-13 is the most widely used barcode in the world. Other codes (even in 2-D) make it possible to include specific information for different activities.

2-D code

Matrix code

Breakthrough Inventions

n the history of technology, there are inventions whose appearance has established a "before" and an "after," radically changing the world and our perception of it. Many of these discoveries, such as the computer and the car, are the realization of dreams and fantasies entertained by humanity for a very long time. Others, such as the Internet and cellular phones, have

CELLULAR PHONE WITH CAMERA
These days, telephones incorporate good quality digital cameras, with screens that can display up to 16 million colors.

changed the way we communicate and have dramatically reduced distances. Breakthroughs such as the microchip and fiber optics have led to tremendous developments in science and art, which in turn have given rise to new technologies. Others, such as the touch screen, have become indispensable tools. ●

The Automobile

Relatively few years have passed since the time of the pioneers who imagined the first "horseless carriages." Yet the automobile has established itself as one of humanity's most fundamental inventions, to the point that today it is impossible to imagine the world without it. Although it has evolved greatly in terms of efficiency and comfort, the operating principle and driving technique have changed very little since 1885, when Karl Benz presented his tricycle powered by an internal combustion engine. ●

A Four-Stroke Cycle

The internal combustion engine converts the chemical energy of the fuel into mechanical energy to move a machine. The motors of modern cars usually operate on a four-stroke cycle.

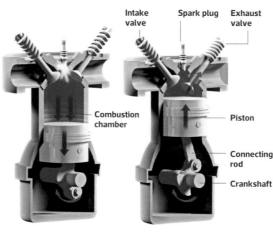

Intake valve   Spark plug   Exhaust valve

Combustion chamber

Piston

Connecting rod

Crankshaft

1st stroke (intake)
The piston descends and the intake valve opens to let in the mixture of fuel and air.

2nd stroke (compression)
When the piston reaches its lowest point, the intake valve closes. The piston then starts the second stroke: as it rises, the fuel-air mixture is compressed.

3rd stroke (combustion)
When the fuel and air reach maximum compression (at which point it becomes highly flammable), a spark produced by the spark plug triggers combustion. The burning gases expand rapidly and push the piston downward, generating power.

4th stroke (exhaust)
The exhaust valve opens to release the combustion gases that are pushed by the piston as it moves upward again. When the piston reaches the top, the exhaust valve closes, the intake valve opens, and the cycle starts again.

25 %

The average efficiency of an internal combustion engine. In other words, only 25% of the chemical energy of the fuel is converted into mechanical energy, though, this varies between fuel sources.

ARRANGEMENT OF THE CYLINDERS

Straight-line arrangement
Engines are simple and efficient in terms of air cooling, but they take up a great deal of space.

V arrangement
Their performance is similar to straight-line engines, but the engine can be smaller or more cylinders can be used in the same space for greater power.

Evolution

 The history of the motor vehicle is packed with milestones, some of the most prominent of which are listed below.

1769
The first self-propelled vehicle is considered to have been designed by the French inventor Nicolas-Joseph Cugnot in 1769. It was steam powered, weighed 2 tons, and reached 5 miles per hour.

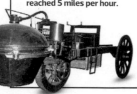

1885
German engineer Karl Benz unveils a tricycle driven by an internal combustion engine. It was the first gasoline-powered motor vehicle.

1908
Henry Ford launches his Ford Model T, the first car to be affordable for the masses. Fifteen million Model Ts were sold worldwide.

1938
The Volkswagen Beetle was released, becoming one of the best-selling cars in history. It was produced between 1938 and 2003, selling 21 million units.

1959
The Volvo Amazon becomes the first car with seatbelts as standard. Three years earlier, Ford had offered seatbelts as an option.

1971
The Lunar Roving Vehicle (LRV) becomes the first motor vehicle to drive on the Moon, during the Apollo 15 mission.

Parts of the Car

Countless electronic, mechanical, and hydraulic devices work together to make modern cars comfortable, reliable, and easy to drive.

Engine
This is where the chemical energy of the fuel is converted into mechanical energy through combustion.

Dashboard
Provides the driver with information such as speed, engine revolutions per minute (RPM), engine temperature, fuel level, oil pressure, and battery charge

Gearbox
Connects the engine with the transmission system via gears, making it possible to increase or decrease the tractive effort and, therefore, the speed. There is also a reverse gear.

Fuel tank
Stores fuel that the engine uses to move the vehicle

Suspension
Absorbs the effect of uneven surfaces with a system of springs and hydraulic shock absorbers

Transmission system
Transfers the mechanical energy generated by the engine to the wheels of the vehicle to set it in motion

Chassis
Provides the automobile with rigidity and structure and supports various devices and systems

Steering system
Connects the steering wheel to the front wheels via gearing systems to steer the vehicle

Brakes
Using discs or bands, they generate friction and stop the wheels.

Batteries
generate the energy needed to start the vehicle and to power systems such as the lights, radio, fuel pump, and so forth. When the vehicle is running, these systems are powered by the alternator.

Radiator
Fresh air passes through its vents to cool the water, or water mixture, that then cools the engine.

Alternative Fuels

Because gasoline is a nonrenewable and polluting resource, research into alternative fuels has been carried out for decades, although very few of these alternatives have taken off on a large scale.

1997

The Thrust SuperSonic breaks the sound barrier, reaching 764 miles per hour, powered by two Rolls Royce jet engines.

Biofuels
These are produced by fermenting crops such as corn, soybeans, or sugarcane. In general, they require only minor engine modifications, which are increasingly being done by manufacturers of new vehicles.

Hydrogen
This is another clean, renewable fuel, although cars that run on hydrogen have limitations in fuel availability, which has limited their use to organizations with their own fueling stations.

Electricity
Like hydrogen, this is a clean, renewable fuel, but these cars have range limitations that have limited their appeal.

Solar energy
This is used in electric cars, powered by energy from the Sun. To date, only experimental prototypes exist.

Skyscrapers

The development of new materials—especially high-performance concrete and steel—has led to the design and construction of buildings to heights never achieved before. For architects and engineers who work on the construction of large skyscrapers, the greatest challenges lie in ensuring the adequate delivery of services, from elevator systems and gas and water lines to complex emergency systems. There is also a new issue to deal with: how to make the structures less vulnerable to potential terrorist attacks, especially after the September 11, 2001, attacks in New York City. ●

The Burj Khalifa

◢ is the tallest building in the world. It is in Dubai, United Arab Emirates. Its final height is 2,722 feet (829 m).

TECHNICAL SPECIFICATIONS

● Height: **2,722 feet (829 m)**

● Floors: **163**

● Elevators: **1,936 feet per minute (590 m/min)** or **22 miles per hour (36 km/h)** (they are the fastest in the world)

● Structure: **High-performance concrete reinforced with steel**

● Exterior: **Glass with solar filters, aluminum, and stainless steel**

● Volume of concrete: **9,181,810 cubic feet (260,000 cu m)**

● Reinforced steel: **34,000 tons (30,844 metric tons)**

● Cost: **$1.5 billion**

● Weight: **500,000 tons without people (452,592 metric tons)**

FLEXIBILITY

Strong winds can cause tall skyscrapers to sway. The Burj Khalifa building, given its height, will be particularly vulnerable to this phenomenon.

Height	Sway
1,985 feet (605 m)	5 feet (1.5 m)
1,870 feet (570 m)	4 feet (1.25 m)
1,450 feet (442 m)	2.5 feet (.75 m)
1,230 feet (375 m)	2 feet (.6 m)

250,000

The number of gallons of water required to supply the daily demand at the Burj Khalifa skyscraper.

From the Ground to the Sky

◢ The construction of a skyscraper begins with the digging of a large pit for the foundation that will support the entire edifice. This structure of concrete and steel has to take into consideration the weight of the building, lateral resistance to winds, and, possibly, earthquakes.

1 The steel and concrete foundation is made up of a series of bases. Each base supports one of the main columns.

The core provides the skyscraper with strong lateral resistance. It is also made of concrete and steel and generally houses service elements (elevators, stairways, etc.).

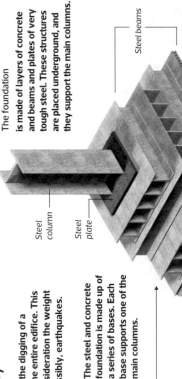

The foundation is made of layers of concrete and beams and plates of very tough steel. These structures are placed underground, and they support the main columns.

Steel beams

Concrete foundation

Steel column

Steel plate

2 The weight of the building rests upon columns made of high-performance, reinforced concrete.

Reinforced concrete is the basic material in modern construction. It consists of a layer of concrete with an internal steel structure that gives it extraordinary resistance.

STRUCTURE

The base of the building is designed in a Y shape. In addition to providing structural strength, this design provides more area for windows. Prior to construction, the structure was rotated according to the prevailing winds to reduce structural stress.

Core

SAMPLE FLOOR PLAN
Distribution of units/rooms

Size of corner units: 1,980 square feet (184 sq m)

Total area (not including hallways and public areas): 22,310 square feet (2,073 sq m)

- ☐ Lobby and service areas
- ☐ Units/rooms
- ☒ Elevators
- ▥ Emergency exits

Joints
The beams and main columns are joined by bolts, welds, rivets, concrete fittings, or a combination of these techniques.

③ The columns together with the beams of steel and concrete form the framework of the skyscraper.

Concrete

High-performance concrete is manufactured by using finer particles and adding special chemicals. Because of its increased resistance, smaller amounts of concrete are needed.

④ Finally, the curtain wall is built over the framework. It is typically made of glass panels, although other materials are also used.

The Tallest in the World

⬆ Today the tallest buildings in the world stand between 980 and 1,640 feet (300–500 m). But the new generation of skyscrapers will at least double this measure.

| Empire State Building (U.S.) 1,250 feet (381 m) | World Trade Center (U.S.) 1,368 feet (417 m) —destroyed in 2001 | Jin Mao Tower (China) 1,377 feet (420 m) | Willis Tower (U.S.) 1,450 feet (442 m) | Petronas Twin Towers (Malaysia) 1,483 feet (452 m) | Taipei 101 (Taiwan) 1,667 feet (508 m) | Burj Khalifa (U.A.E.) 2,722 feet (829 m) |

The Uncertain Primacy of the Burj Khalifa

The record set by Burj Khalifa could be short-lived if the planned construction of the Al Burj, also in Dubai and with a planned height of 3,940 feet (1,200 m), goes forward.

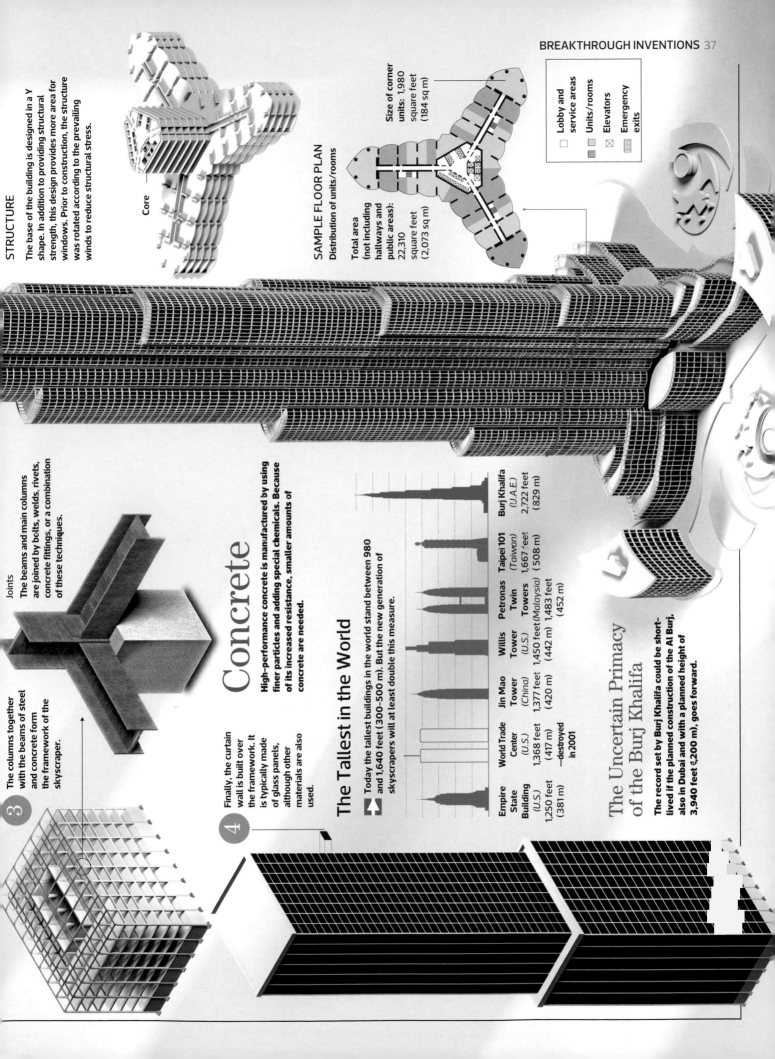

The Microchip

iny as it is, the microchip is the brain of computerized systems, the intelligence that makes all the computer's components function in a coordinated way. The first microchip appeared almost 60 years ago, and since then its capabilities have constantly increased while its components have shrunk to a microscopic size. Specialists are currently working to develop molecular devices that will take the potential of machines to levels that are unimaginable today.

The Smallest Brain in the World

 Millions of components forming the most complex integrated circuits developed by humanity are assembled in a space of just a few square millimeters. Microprocessors work on the basis of "logic gates" in a "language" written in long sequences of two numbers: ones and zeros. The difference between a one and zero may simply be the presence or absence of an electric current.

6,000

The number of calculations per second that could be handled by the Intel 4004 processor, considered to be the first microprocessor. Present-day processors can carry out thousands of millions of calculations per second.

0.12 inch (3 mm)

0.20 inch (5 mm)

The Hall of Fame

 In general, the efficiency and capabilities of computers multiply each time a new microprocessor appears on the market. However, some of them have represented genuine milestones in the history of computers.

1971	1975	1976	1978	1985
Intel 4004	**MOS 6502**	**Zilog Z80**	**Intel 8086**	**Intel 80386**
The first microprocessor with a single chip to come onto the market. The 4-bit Intel 4004 was manufactured until 1974 and was succeeded by Intel 8008, with 3,200 transistors.	It caused a revolution when it first appeared on the market in terms of capabilities and price. The MOS 6502 and its immediate descendants formed part of the Atari video games console for the celebrated Apple II and the highly successful Commodore 64.	This 8-bit microprocessor was the most popular chip in the 1980s, when it became the brain of the Spectrum and Sinclair home computers—many people's first contact with the world of computers.	With its 16 bits and 29,000 transistors, this was the first processor based on the architecture known as x86, possibly the most successful of all those used in the history of microprocessors, becoming the brain of the famous IBM PCs.	Also known as i386 and with 275,000 transistors, this was the first 32-bit microprocessor. It was to prove revolutionary, especially with regard to its ability to multitask, which made it a commercial success.

Miniature Circuits

▶ This very thin chip contains an enormous number (in the region of thousands of millions) of interconnected microelectronic devices, mainly diodes and transistors, as well as passive components such as resistors and condensers.

Microcircuits
Made up of thousands of tracks, they determine how an electric current moves within the microprocessor.

Substrate
Acts as a base and insulation for the microprocessor's circuits

Connection points
indicate the points where the circuits connect with the components located on the other side of the substrate.

Tracks

18 months

The time it takes for technology to double the number of transistors on a microprocessor, according to Moore's Law, which has proved fairly accurate to date.

Microprocessor connectors
join the microprocessor to the network of PGA connectors via microscopic wires.

Network of PGA connectors
Inserted in the base of the motherboard CPU, they act as bridges between the microchip and the base plate.

32

The number of cores in a processor cdeveloped by Intel,, which was released in 2010.

Microprocessor

Base of the motherboard

1993

Intel Pentium

Its arrival sent shockwaves through the market, promising as it did to exceed the capabilities of its predecessor, the i486, by an average of five times. It also has its place in history as the first processor that Intel named with a word instead of numbers, for
marketing reasons.

2006

Intel Core Duo

It has two execution cores for improved multitasking. With 151 million transistors, it is the first Intel processor to be used in Apple Mac computers.

The Nanochip

▶ Although it is almost impossible to guess what the capabilities of the chips of the future might be, the trend is toward devices with capabilities thousands of times greater than those of today's chips.

Intel 45 nm

On the subject of component miniaturization, Intel announced in 2007 that it was developing a transistor measuring just 45 nanometers, that is, 2,000 times thinner that a human hair. Furthermore, this latest wonder would be able to repeat on-off cycles (ones and zeros) around 300,000 million times per second. In the future, entire nanometric-sized components in processors will increase the current capabilities of computers by millions.

The Computer

Although it was conceived as a laboratory instrument for carrying out complex calculations, in the 21st century the computer has become a fundamental part of people's lives. Computers have apparently infinite applications, covering everything from industrial processes to services, communication to entertainment. With the emergence of the Internet, e-mail, and laptops in the 1990s, computers became even more important to our society. These three pillars of the globalized world could not exist without computers. ●

Inside a PC

A PC unit houses a labyrinth of cables, chips and circuits which are indecipherable to the average person. However, each part is clearly unique and carries out a specific function, albeit in connection with the other parts.

POWER SUPLY
Receives energy from an external sources and supplies it to the computer. The power supply has a dedicated fan to prevent overheating.

CENTRAL PROCESSING UNIT (CPU)
The computer's brain. The CPU interprets instructions and processes information, either from data that is input into it or data stored in the storage units. It is protected by a fan, which keeps it cool.

VIDEO CARD
This electronic device enables certain information that is managed and processed by the computer to be displayed on a video device, such as a monitor. It also houses the connection port for this monitor.

HARD DRIVE
This is where the computer stores information on a permanent basis, using a system of digital magnetic recording.

Monitor

Images are the result of combining many tiny cells, called "pixels". They use red, green, and blue light to display images, combining them as necessary to create other colors.

27 metric tons

The weight of ENIAC, considered to be the first computer. It was able to solve 5,000 sums and 360 multiplications in 1 second.

Mouse

It controls the cursor's movement on the graphical user interface. It registers movement, calculates the change in coordinates, and moves the cursor on the screen.

Keyboard

Similar to a typewriter, the keyboard allows data (numbers, letters, symbols) to be entered by sending coded signals to the microprocessor.

By pushing a key, the contact is established.

Key
Spring
Conductive
Printed circuit

How a Computer Works

A basic action routes information throughout the computer's components.

Connectors for integrated peripherals
These ports allow external devices such as the keyboard, mouse, speakers, etc. to be connected.

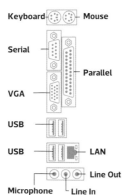

Keyboard — Mouse

Serial

Parallel

VGA

USB

USB — LAN

Line Out

Microphone — Line In

1

Input
Data enters the computer through a keyboard, mouse, or modem and is interpreted by the appropriate circuit.

2

Microprocessor
Controls all computer functions. It processes the entered data and carries out the necessary arithmetic and logic calculations.

3

RAM
(Random Access Memory)
Temporarily stores all the information and programs used by the microprocessor.

4

Processing
Data can travel back and forth from the CPU to the RAM several times until processing is complete.

5

Storage
Data is sent to a storage device, for example, the hard drive.

6

Output
The information on the monitor is updated through the video card.

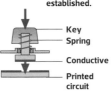

The Internet

I n a worldwide network where interconnected computers of every type exchange information, the social impact of the Internet is comparable to the invention of the printing press, enabling the free flow of information and access to it from anywhere in the world. With the appearance of blogs, the digital world of editing and journalism has become more democratic and inclusive, since virtually anyone can publish their own texts, images, and opinions. ●

HOW IT IS SET UP

The Internet is a worldwide network in which one participates through a service provider, which receives, saves, and distributes information using its computer "server." The user's computer connects to the Internet using a variety of methods, programs, and devices.

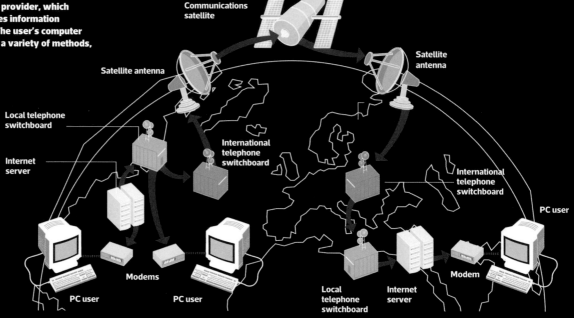

Communications satellite

Satellite antenna

Satellite antenna

Local telephone switchboard

International telephone switchboard

Internet server

International telephone switchboard

PC user

Modems

Modem

PC user

PC user

Local telephone switchboard

Internet server

THE BROWSER

is a program that allows the user to see documents on the World Wide Web and to go from one document to another using the hypertext transfer protocol (HTTP). The most common browsers are Google Chrome, Firefox, and Safari.

A WEBSITE OR WEB PAGE

contains a series of documents written in hypertext markup language (HTML) combined with other, more sophisticated languages, such as Java and Flash animation.

ELECTRONIC MAIL

travels from one computer or device to another through e-mail servers. It can carry attachments, such as photos or text documents.

SEARCH ENGINES

are tools used to find information available on the World Wide Web. They function like a database that is constantly being updated by robots that prowl the Web and collect information. The most commonly used search engines are Google and Yahoo; they also offer other services to their users, such as e-mail and news updates.

CHAT

This service allows a group of users to communicate with each other in real time. It started out only in written form, but it is now possible to transmit audio and video images via webcams through services such as Skype.

VOICE OVER IP

is a system that allows a computer to communicate with a regular telephone anywhere in the world, bypassing normal telephone charges. It requires an Internet connection and a program that enables this type of communication.

Transmitting Information

These interconnected systems share information internally and with external users, forming networks. Information travels from one computer to another through such a network.

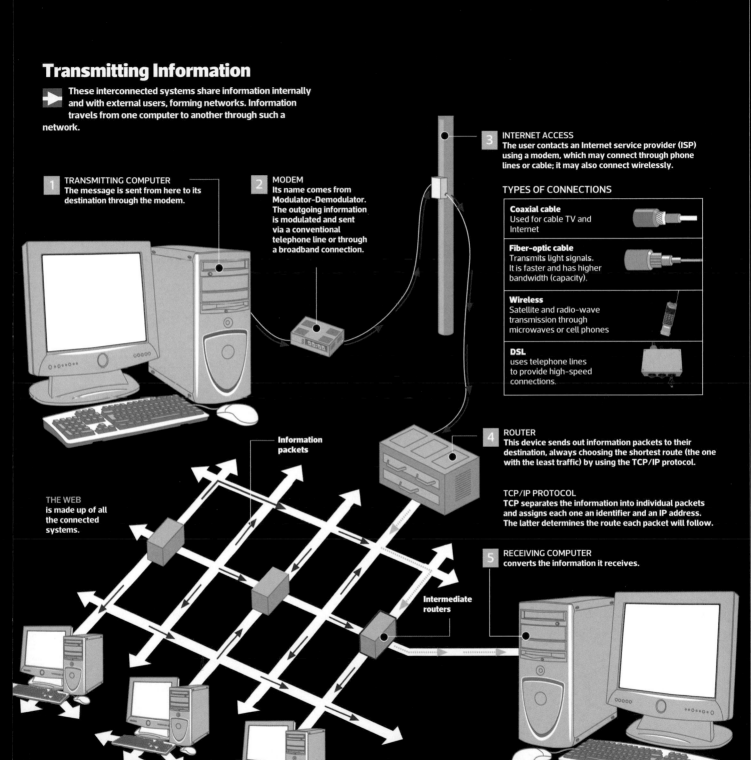

1 TRANSMITTING COMPUTER
The message is sent from here to its destination through the modem.

2 MODEM
Its name comes from Modulator–Demodulator. The outgoing information is modulated and sent via a conventional telephone line or through a broadband connection.

3 INTERNET ACCESS
The user contacts an Internet service provider (ISP) using a modem, which may connect through phone lines or cable; it may also connect wirelessly.

TYPES OF CONNECTIONS

Coaxial cable
Used for cable TV and Internet

Fiber-optic cable
Transmits light signals. It is faster and has higher bandwidth (capacity).

Wireless
Satellite and radio-wave transmission through microwaves or cell phones

DSL
uses telephone lines to provide high-speed connections.

Information packets

THE WEB
is made up of all the connected systems.

4 ROUTER
This device sends out information packets to their destination, always choosing the shortest route (the one with the least traffic) by using the TCP/IP protocol.

TCP/IP PROTOCOL
TCP separates the information into individual packets and assigns each one an identifier and an IP address. The latter determines the route each packet will follow.

5 RECEIVING COMPUTER
converts the information it receives.

Intermediate routers

The Cellular Telephone

Few inventions have had as widespread an impact as the cellular phone. In just three-and-a-half decades, the cellular phone has become extremely popular around the world and almost indispensable for populations in the developed world, to the point that sales already surpass one billion units a year. The latest cell phones, in addition to being small, portable, and light, are true workstations that far exceed their original function of keeping the user connected at any time and place.

Communication

Providers divide an area into a system of cell sites. Each site has an antenna that detects the presence of a particular cell phone in its area and identifies it through the phone's unique code.

2 The switch

The switch maintains a database of all the cell phones that are turned on and their cell-site locations. It then locates the position of the called party and sends the information to the appropriate cell site.

1 Calling

When a number is dialed, the antenna at the local cell site identifies the caller and the called party. It then transmits this information to the switch.

28 ounces (780 g)

was the weight of the Motorola DynaTAC 8000X, which was the first commercially available cellular phone. More recent models weigh less than 2 ounces (50 g). The latest iPhone 7 weighs 4.87 ounces (138 g) lighter than the heaviest 6S model.

The Evolution of the Cell Phone

Since the first cell phone appeared on the market in 1983, mobile telephones have become smaller and, at the same time, they have incorporated dozens of new features, such as touch screens, Internet access, picture taking, videoconferencing and downloading popular Apps such as Snapchat, Instagram and Twitter; mobile phones also store and play music, movies, games, and more.

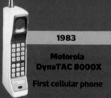

1983
Motorola DynaTAC 8000X
First cellular phone

1993
Simon Personal Communicator
First PDA/cell phone Added applications such as a calculator, calendar, address book, etc.

1996
Motorola StarTAC
First clamshell cell phone Design reaches the cell phone

1999
Nokia 7110
One of the first to use Wireless Application Protocol (WAP)

1999
Sharp J-SH04
First cell-phone camera (released only in Japan)

2000
Samsung SCH-M105
First MP3 cell phone

2001
Kyocera QCP6035
First Palm-powered cell phone

In Motion

Cell sites detect the movement of a cell phone; as the signal weakens at one site, it becomes stronger at another. This movement allows seamless communication, even during high-speed movement from one cell site to another.

When a cell phone user moves away from the service provider's network, the service can be provided by another carrier. The phone is then in roaming mode.

INTERNATIONAL CALLS

As is the case with landline phones, international communications are facilitated with the assistance of satellites.

Smartphones

In addition to being a telephone and having such traditional features as a calendar, calculator, and camera, a smartphone incorporates advanced computing capabilities for connecting to the Internet through Wi-Fi and to other devices through Bluetooth.

3 Connecting

The local cell-site antenna establishes communication with the requested cell phone.

6.8 billion

is the approximate number of cell phones in use in the world, according to the latest data. This number is less than 1 billion short of the entire world's population.

2001

Panasonic P2101V

Among the first third-generation cell phones (with videoconferencing)

2005

Motorola ROKR

First cell phone with iTunes

2007

iPhone

has a 3.5-inch (8.9-cm) touch screen and Wi-Fi Web access.

Fiber Optics

A few simple basic optical principles allowed researchers to develop one of today's most widespread and efficient systems for transporting information. Optical fiber is not only more economical, lighter, and more versatile than traditional copper wire, but it also allows a much greater and faster flow of data, which travels through filaments the thickness of a human hair, converted into pulses of light. Medicine is another of the fields in which fiber optics has made significant advances, allowing formerly invasive operations and examinations to be carried out with a minimum of suffering for patients.

An "Illuminated" Cable

A phenomenon known as "total reflection" allows light to travel through a fine glass or plastic tube (the fiber), covering great distances with limited loss. The fibers can also be bundled together to form cables.

TOTAL REFLECTION

This is an optical phenomenon that occurs between two substances with different refractive indices and also depends on the angle of incidence of a beam of light.

In the first case, a beam crosses one medium (for example, water) and enters another (for example, air). This produces the phenomenon of refraction (like when you dip a pencil into a glass of water and it appears to bend).

In the second case, when the beam of light exceeds a "critical angle" of incidence the phenomenon of "total reflection" takes place. The light bounces back, as if from a mirror.

THE OPTICAL FIBER

The optical fiber basically consists of a core of glass or plastic, with an outer layer of a similar material, but with a lower refractive index.

Core

Outer layer

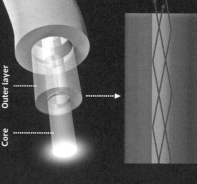

Within the optical fiber, the light bounces off the walls of the core as a result of total reflection, with almost zero loss, and can therefore travel great distances, transmitting information.

0.004 inch
(0.1 mm)

The approximate thickness of an optical fiber, comparable to a human hair.

The Light's Journey

The transmission of data through the optical fiber really begins with an electric signal that is converted into light and is then converted back into an electric signal at the end of its journey.

1 A computer, telephone, radio, or TV station generates a binary or analog electric signal.

2 An encoder interprets the signal and transforms it into light signals with the help of a diode (an LED or laser).

3 The pulses of light generated by the diode are relayed through the fiber-optic cable.

4 Because the signal loses intensity with distance, but its characteristics do not deteriorate, optical amplifiers located at specific distances in the cable amplify the signal.

5 A photodiode captures the light signals at the end of the cable, and a decoder turns them back into electric, analog, or digital signals before they arrive at the receiver (TV, computer, telephone, etc.).

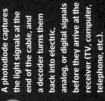

Air Is Better

Recent research has shown that waves of light may encounter less resistance when traveling through a hollow core. This would reduce the need for optical amplifiers.

Solid core

When the core is solid, made of glass for instance, the light signal progressively loses intensity. This is what happens in traditional optical fibers.

Hollow core

If the core were hollow and the cladding consisted of alternate layers of glass and air, the structure could reflect the lost beams and send them back to the core, strengthening the signal.

Other Applications

Telecommunications is undoubtedly the area in which the use of optical fibers is most widespread. However, they are used in a number of other fields.

Medicine

Ultra-fine instruments can be made from strands of optical fiber and lenses, making it possible to examine objects through a small hole. These are known as endoscopes, and they help make diagnostic or surgical operations as noninvasive as possible for patients.

Industry

Endoscopes also have numerous industrial applications. Their ability to bend makes it possible to guide a beam of light to a point outside of the line of vision.

Entertainment

Special lighting effects and a wide range of decorations employ optical fibers.

24,000 miles
(39,000 km)

The length of SEA-ME-WE 3, the longest fiber-optic cable in the world, which connects the Far East and Southeast Asia with the Middle East, Africa, and Europe

The Touch Screen

Although the technology underlying the development of touch screens is very old—the theoretical possibility of constructing them existed five decades ago—it is only in the last two decades that these ingenious devices have become widespread in use. This explosion is largely the result of the development of small personal devices such as cellular phones and electronic organizers, where a keyboard is replaced outright. Today, the iPhone, tablet and e-reader industries have developed touch screens that allow more than one "touch" at a time, dragging an object to operate a computer, selecting options from a menu, and even drawing. ●

A Multi-touch Display

Normally, touch screens allow only one touch at a time. However, with the launch of Apple's iPhone, users can now benefit from a screen that allows various simultaneous touches. This technology is based on an electric phenomenon known as "capacitance" and the use of a layer of electrodes on which each device functions as a coordinate point.

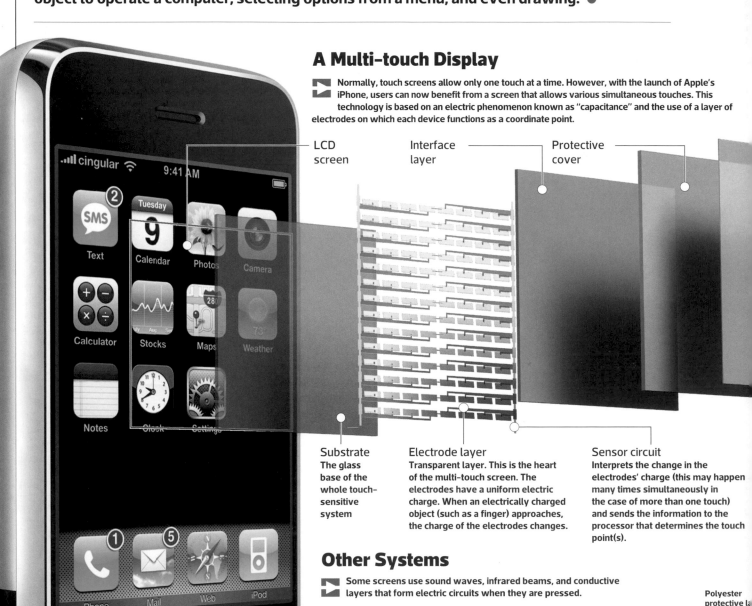

LCD screen

Interface layer

Protective cover

Substrate
The glass base of the whole touch-sensitive system

Electrode layer
Transparent layer. This is the heart of the multi-touch screen. The electrodes have a uniform electric charge. When an electrically charged object (such as a finger) approaches, the charge of the electrodes changes.

Sensor circuit
Interprets the change in the electrodes' charge (this may happen many times simultaneously in the case of more than one touch) and sends the information to the processor that determines the touch point(s).

Other Systems

Some screens use sound waves, infrared beams, and conductive layers that form electric circuits when they are pressed.

RESISTIVE SCREEN

This is the most widespread, robust, and economical method. Two conductive layers separated by insulating gaps come into contact when they are pressed (the touch on the screen). The system calculates the point of contact and even, in some cases, the pressure. Resistive screens are generally found in machines that control industrial processes and in Palm Pilots.

Polyester protective la

LCD screen

Conductive layers

Glass screen

Resistive layer

A Touch of Complexity

 It takes just the slightest touch on the screen of an iPhone to trigger a complex electric and mathematical mechanism that determines the position of contact on the screen and the function to be activated.

1
The screen registers the touch.

2
The raw data is collected.

3
The interference is removed.

4
The system calculates the degree of touch pressure.

5
A "touch area" is established.

6
Finally, the system calculates the exact coordinates of the contact.

On capacitance touch screens, such as that of the iPhone, the touches must be made with an electrically charged object. If a neutral object such as a piece of plastic is used, the screen does not detect the touch.

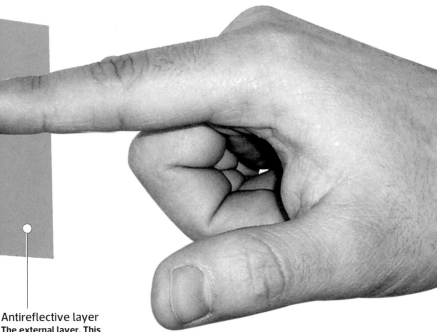

Antireflective layer
The external layer. This must be robust, as it is the part that is touched and exposed to dust and the environment in general.

0.05 inch (1.16 mm)

THE THICKNESS OF THE IPHONE'S MULTI-TOUCH SCREEN

SURFACE ACOUSTIC WAVE SCREEN

The screen is covered by a layer of ultrasound waves. When an object touches the screen, the ultrasound layer is interrupted, and the system detects the position of the interference. These are generally found in vending machines and cash machines.

 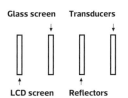

Glass screen **Transducers**

LCD screen **Reflectors**

Applications

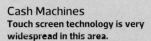 Where it is necessary to input data into a system without the aid of a keyboard, touch screens play an ever more important role. Some examples include the following:

Microsoft Surface
This is a computer in the form of a table, launched in 2007, on which it is possible to carry out an infinite number of activities and tasks without a keyboard. It has a multi-touch screen based on a technology that uses five cameras with devices that detect close infrared.

Digitizing Tablets
These are not exactly touch screens, but they allow designers and illustrators to "draw" on a tablet with a magnetic pencil and see the results instantly on a monitor. The tablet contains a network of conductive fibers that receive stimuli from the magnetic tip of the pencil.

Cash Machines
Touch screen technology is very widespread in this area.

Palm Pilot
The use of touch screens makes it possible to input data and commands at high speeds without the need for a keyboard, which would be particularly unsuitable for this type of small device.

Pros and Cons

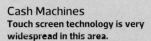 The ideal touch screen technology has yet to be developed. For the time being, each of the various systems presents some advantages and disadvantages.

	Advantages	Disadvantages
Resistive	The cheapest option	Brightness varies model to model
	Can be touched with any object	Can be damaged by sharp objects
	High resolution and accuracy	
Capacitive	High clarity and resolution	Can only be touched by electrically charged objects or conductors in contact with a charged object. Requires heavy swipes.
	Very durable; difficult to damage	
		Can require calibration
Ultrasound	Excellent resolution, precision, sensitivity	Expensive
	Responds to the touch of any object	Affected by grease, water, and dust in the atmosphere

Science and Health

There was a time when medicine was a rudimentary science that used a few basic tools to heal patients. However, in just 500 years, thanks to remarkable scientific and technical advances, medicine has become a technological discipline. Scientific developments have significantly extended human life expectancy, and treatments that would have

SURGICAL CLIP
Made of an alloy of nickel
and titanium, this minute
computer-assisted clamp is
used in the removal of tumors
from the head or neck.

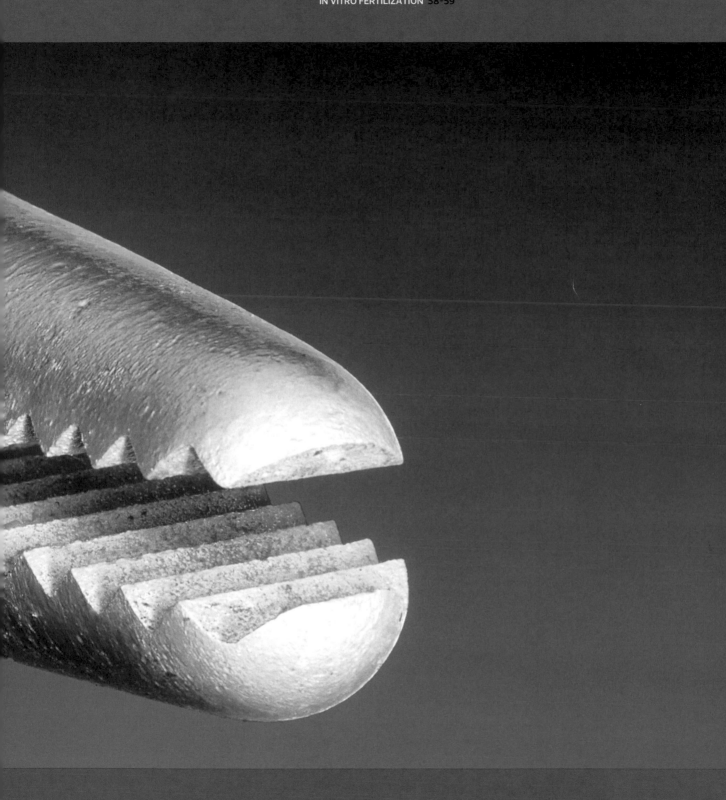

been considered miracles in the past are now commonplace. Obviously, the story does not end here: a great deal remains to be done, but advances such as robotic surgery, where a surgeon can work from a virtual reality simulator many miles away, and magnetic resonance equipment, which can detect soft-tissue tumors, are extremely important. ●

Magnetic Resonance Imaging (MRI)

T hanks to a sophisticated technology that combines magnetic fields and radio waves, it is possible to render high-quality images of soft tissue in the human body without inconvenience to the patient, other than the requirement for the patient to remain still for a few minutes. Another revolutionary feature of this technique is that it does not require the use of contrast agents or the use of x-rays, as is the case for radiography or computerized tomography. ●

Water molecule

O

H

Inside a Scanner

▶ To render an image of the soft tissue in the human body, the machine scans for the hydrogen atoms in these tissues. To detect the atoms, the area is initially subjected to a powerful magnetic field and later stimulated using radio-frequency waves. This process causes the atoms to release energy that is then detected by the scanner and converted into images.

Superconducting magnet

The magnet, made out of a niobium–titanium alloy, becomes a superconductor when it is cooled to –452° F (–269° C). It generates a powerful magnetic field that lines up the hydrogen protons prior to their being stimulated with the radio waves.

Cooling systems

In addition to compensating for the enormous amounts of heat generated by the electromagnetic equipment, these systems cool the main magnet to –452° F (–269° C) to turn it into a superconductor. Liquid helium is generally used as the cooling agent.

Magnetic gradient coils

It generate secondary magnetic fields that, together with the superconducting magnet, enable imaging of different planes of the human body.

Radio-frequency transmitter

It emits radio signals through a transmitting coil (antenna) to stimulate the hydrogen atoms that are aligned by the magnetic field. When the stimulation stops, the atoms release energy that is captured and used to form the image.

HYDROGEN IN THE BODY

Hydrogen atoms are present in almost all tissues and fluids, especially in water (which makes up 70 percent of the body) and in fat.

The hydrogen atom

is the simplest element of nature.
It has just one proton (+) and one electron (–).

Electron

H

+

Proton

Because of its physical structure, the hydrogen atom's proton spins on its axis. This generates a magnetic field that will interact with an external magnetic field.

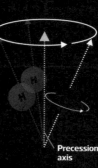

+

Proton

Rotation

–

A magnetic dipole is created along the axis of rotation.

Magnetic field

It also spins around a second axis, like a top, traveling within a conelike (precession) trajectory.

Precession axis

Classification

Low-energy nuclei. The spin and the precession axis rotate in the same direction.

High-energy nuclei. The spin and the precession axis rotate in opposite directions.

Planes

▶ Magnetic resonance imaging can generate cross-sectional images at any point in the human body and in any plane.

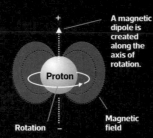

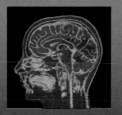

Profile cross section

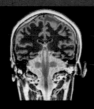

Frontal cross section

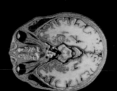

Top cross section

High Magnetism

The magnetic field generated by MRI scanners tends to be tens of thousands of times more powerful than the magnetic field of the Earth.

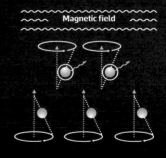

HUNTING FOR ATOMS

1 Hydrogen in the body

The axes of precession are randomly oriented in different directions.

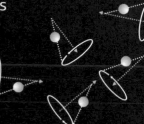

2 Magnetism

A strong magnetic field helps to line up the precession axes in the same direction.

Magnetic field

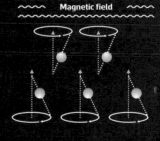

3 Stimulation

Next, energy in the form of radio waves is applied, and low-energy protons absorb it to become high-energy protons.

Magnetic field

Radio waves

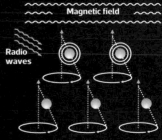

4 Relaxation

When transmission of radio waves stops, the low-energy protons return to their previous state. While they relax, they release the energy they have absorbed.

Magnetic field

5 Analysis

This released energy is interpreted by the MRI scanner to form images.

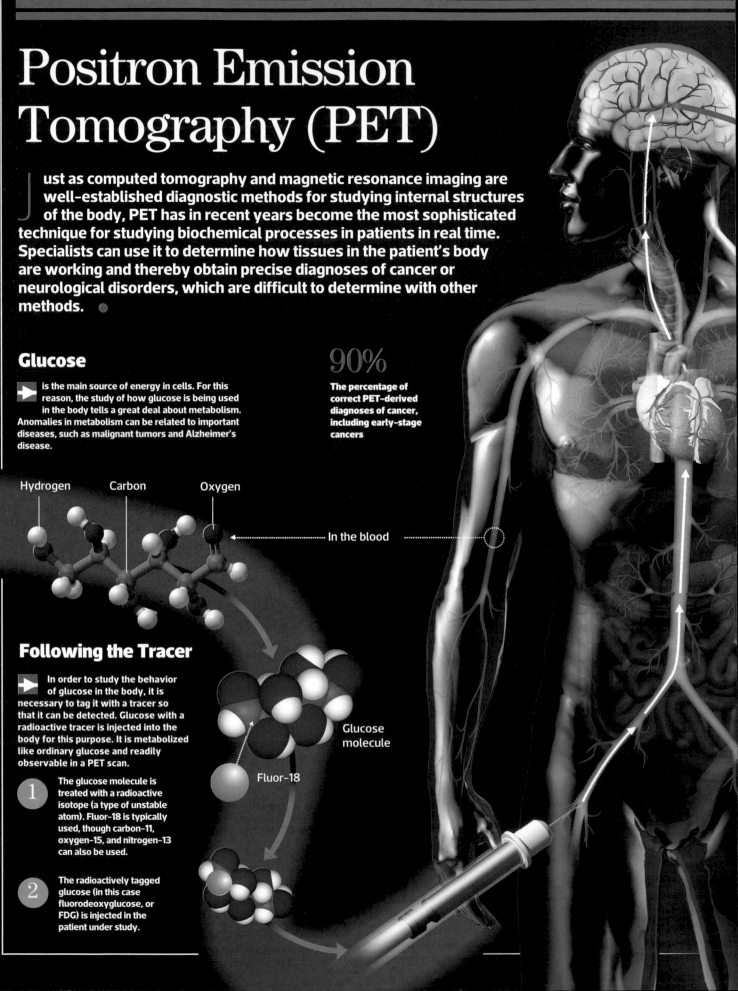

Positron Emission Tomography (PET)

J ust as computed tomography and magnetic resonance imaging are well-established diagnostic methods for studying internal structures of the body, PET has in recent years become the most sophisticated technique for studying biochemical processes in patients in real time. Specialists can use it to determine how tissues in the patient's body are working and thereby obtain precise diagnoses of cancer or neurological disorders, which are difficult to determine with other methods.

Glucose

is the main source of energy in cells. For this reason, the study of how glucose is being used in the body tells a great deal about metabolism. Anomalies in metabolism can be related to important diseases, such as malignant tumors and Alzheimer's disease.

90%

The percentage of correct PET-derived diagnoses of cancer, including early-stage cancers

Hydrogen   Carbon   Oxygen

In the blood

Following the Tracer

In order to study the behavior of glucose in the body, it is necessary to tag it with a tracer so that it can be detected. Glucose with a radioactive tracer is injected into the body for this purpose. It is metabolized like ordinary glucose and readily observable in a PET scan.

1 The glucose molecule is treated with a radioactive isotope (a type of unstable atom). Fluor-18 is typically used, though carbon-11, oxygen-15, and nitrogen-13 can also be used.

2 The radioactively tagged glucose (in this case fluorodeoxyglucose, or FDG) is injected in the patient under study.

Glucose molecule

Fluor-18

Luminous Collision

Once FDG is inside the body of the patient, it emits positrons as it is absorbed and metabolized. Thanks to the emission of positrons, the process can be followed in a PET scan.

Glucose molecule

3 Within the FDG molecule, fluor-18 emits positrons, which are the antimatter equivalent of electrons. In other words, positrons are electrons that have a positive instead of a negative charge.

Positron

Fluor-18

Gamma rays

Electron

Positron

Gamma rays

Electron

4 In the rest of the tissues and structures of the body, there are many free electrons that are susceptible to encountering positrons emitted by the FDG.

5 When an electron (with a negative charge) collides with a positron (with a positive charge), both particles are annihilated and all their mass changes into energy. More precisely, the mass changes into two gamma-ray photons that are emitted in opposite directions, at 180º from each other.

6 These flashes are captured and amplified in the PET scan to determine the position and concentration of FDG molecules and to track them within the patient's body. The PET scan processor then converts this information into color images.

SIEMENS

ECAT

Photon amplifier

0.2 inch (5 mm)

The minimum resolution of a PET scan. Malignant tumors that are smaller than this cannot be detected by this technique.

Images

PET scans are very useful for diagnosing malignant tumors and neurological pathologies, such as Alzheimer's disease or Parkinson's disease. Whereas computed tomography can provide anatomical and structural information for internal organs, a PET scan can provide information about metabolic and biochemical activity and how medicines act.

NORMAL

This image shows the metabolic activity of a normal brain. The nerve cells consume large amounts of glucose.

WITH ALZHEIMER'S DISEASE

This image clearly shows areas that are completely dark, indicating the low level of glucose metabolism that is characteristic of Alzheimer's disease.

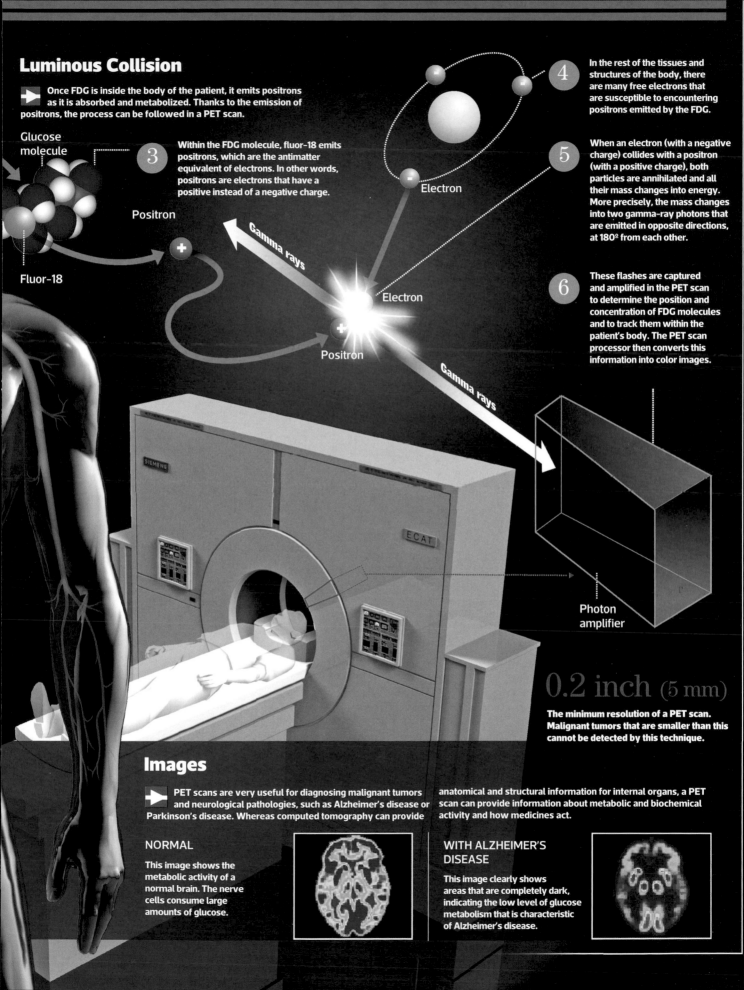

4-D Ultrasound

As the latest word in diagnostic examinations in obstetrics, ultrasound imaging in four dimensions incorporates time as a new variable, and it produces color images in real time that give the impression of watching a movie of a baby as it is growing inside the uterus. However, it is not a movie, properly speaking, but the sweep of ultrasonic waves that are reflected as echoes by the fetus. These echoes are analyzed and converted into images by powerful processors that perform mathematical calculations. The use of 4-D ultrasound has not yet been completely embraced by doctors, many of whom still use traditional two-dimensional ultrasounds for their exams. ●

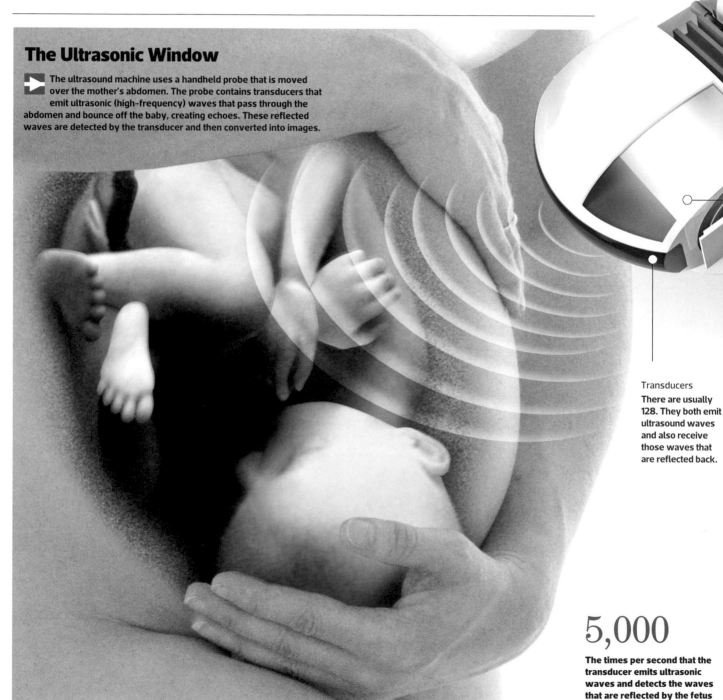

The Ultrasonic Window

The ultrasound machine uses a handheld probe that is moved over the mother's abdomen. The probe contains transducers that emit ultrasonic (high-frequency) waves that pass through the abdomen and bounce off the baby, creating echoes. These reflected waves are detected by the transducer and then converted into images.

Transducers
There are usually 128. They both emit ultrasound waves and also receive those waves that are reflected back.

5,000

The times per second that the transducer emits ultrasonic waves and detects the waves that are reflected by the fetus

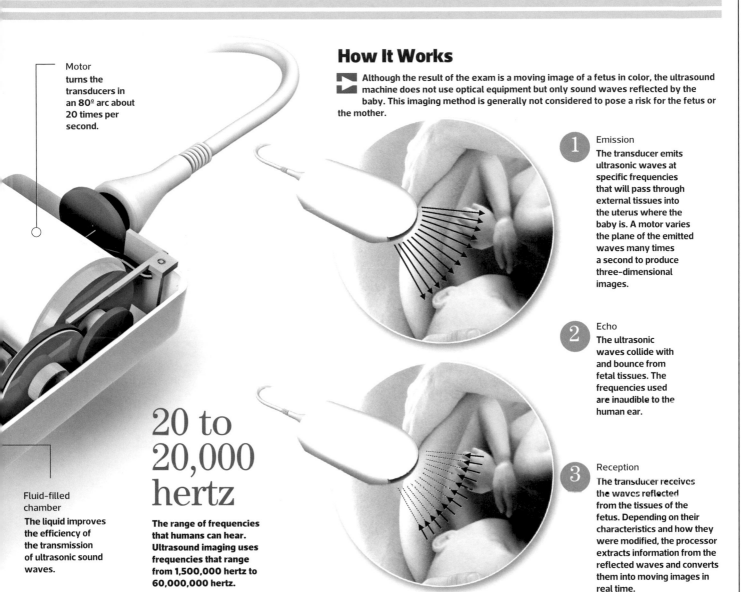

Motor
turns the transducers in an 80º arc about 20 times per second.

Fluid-filled chamber
The liquid improves the efficiency of the transmission of ultrasonic sound waves.

20 to 20,000 hertz

The range of frequencies that humans can hear. Ultrasound imaging uses frequencies that range from 1,500,000 hertz to 60,000,000 hertz.

How It Works

Although the result of the exam is a moving image of a fetus in color, the ultrasound machine does not use optical equipment but only sound waves reflected by the baby. This imaging method is generally not considered to pose a risk for the fetus or the mother.

1 Emission
The transducer emits ultrasonic waves at specific frequencies that will pass through external tissues into the uterus where the baby is. A motor varies the plane of the emitted waves many times a second to produce three-dimensional images.

2 Echo
The ultrasonic waves collide with and bounce from fetal tissues. The frequencies used are inaudible to the human ear.

3 Reception
The transducer receives the waves reflected from the tissues of the fetus. Depending on their characteristics and how they were modified, the processor extracts information from the reflected waves and converts them into moving images in real time.

Development

Ultrasound imaging technology has developed in recent years from producing somewhat confusing multicolored pictures to movielike images of the fetus in the uterus.

2-D ULTRASOUND

is for obstetrics the ultrasound-imaging method par excellence. Although it is much less spectacular than more modern methods, doctors prefer it because it provides cross-sectional views of the fetus from any angle, which is helpful in examining its internal structures.

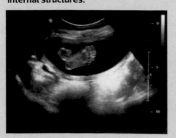

3-D ULTRASOUND

yields a static three-dimensional image of the fetus. It can be used to identify structural malformations and even facial features. The image is produced by obtaining a series of parallel cross-sectional views along the length of the fetus. These views are then processed mathematically to produce the three-dimensional image.

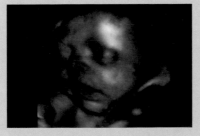

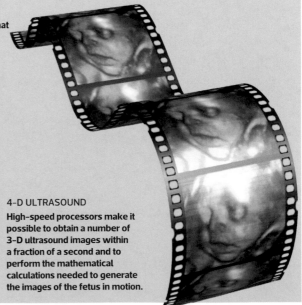

4-D ULTRASOUND

High-speed processors make it possible to obtain a number of 3-D ultrasound images within a fraction of a second and to perform the mathematical calculations needed to generate the images of the fetus in motion.

In Vitro Fertilization

ver since the first successful case of in vitro fertilization in the United Kingdom almost four decades ago, this technique has become the most popular and widespread method of assisted reproductive technology. It involves removing a woman's ova, or eggs, and fertilizing them with sperm outside the woman's womb; in fact, the procedure is done in a laboratory to avoid various problems that can hinder a natural pregnancy. Once fertilized, the embryo is implanted in the uterus to continue gestation. Over time, in vitro fertilization techniques have become more efficient, and in the past few years, the number of successful pregnancies has seen a seven-fold increase. Today in vitro fertilization can be combined with other techniques to increase the chances of conception.

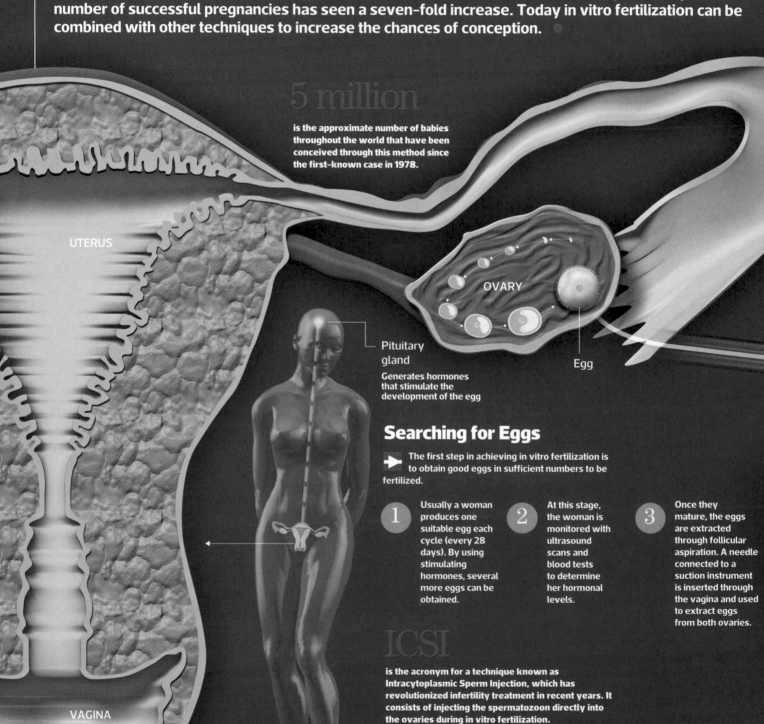

5 million

is the approximate number of babies throughout the world that have been conceived through this method since the first-known case in 1978.

UTERUS

OVARY

Egg

Pituitary gland
Generates hormones that stimulate the development of the egg

Searching for Eggs

The first step in achieving in vitro fertilization is to obtain good eggs in sufficient numbers to be fertilized.

1 Usually a woman produces one suitable egg each cycle (every 28 days). By using stimulating hormones, several more eggs can be obtained.

2 At this stage, the woman is monitored with ultrasound scans and blood tests to determine her hormonal levels.

3 Once they mature, the eggs are extracted through follicular aspiration. A needle connected to a suction instrument is inserted through the vagina and used to extract eggs from both ovaries.

ICSI

is the acronym for a technique known as Intracytoplasmic Sperm Injection, which has revolutionized infertility treatment in recent years. It consists of injecting the spermatozoon directly into the ovaries during in vitro fertilization.

VAGINA

A Baby Factory

Once the most suitable eggs are selected, they are fertilized in a laboratory with the sperm of the future father and either inserted into the mother's uterus or frozen for use at a later time.

The semen sample obtained from the father is treated to separate the spermatozoa and to select the best ones.

The head of the spermatozoon contains DNA that, in combination with the egg's DNA, will create a new life.

Back into the Uterus

UTERUS

Implantation

The selected embryos (usually several are selected to increase the chances of success) are transferred to the mother's uterus through a catheter inserted into the vagina.

Days 6 to 18

Trophoblast
Outer cells develop the placenta.

Embryoblast
Inner cells develop the fetus.

Fertilization

takes place in a special cultivation medium in a petri dish at the same temperature as the human body.

The embryo

From this moment, the embryo is monitored and cared for by medical personnel. If it develops successfully, it will become a baby.

After 12 hours

the first cellular division takes place. The embryo now consists of two cells. The number of cells increases exponentially every 12 to 15 hours.

Day 3

When the embryo reaches between 16 and 64 cells, it is called a morula (from the Latin word *morus*, meaning "mulberry").

Day 5

When it surpasses 64 cells, the embryo becomes a blastula. A large cavity forms in the middle. At this phase, the embryo can be transferred to the woman's uterus.

Success Rates

of in vitro fertilization are determined by different factors, including the age of a patient's eggs.

For a 35-year-old woman, statistics show that only one of every 16 eggs will develop and result in a pregnancy.

Five eggs are not suitable.

Five eggs will not be fertilized.

Between one and six implanted eggs could produce a baby.

Bionic Implants

ntil a few decades ago, the only option for amputees was the use of rigid and uncomfortable wood prostheses. Today at the beginning of the 21st century, the dream of being able to use artificial limbs that are connected through the nervous system—with the capability of responding to direct commands from the brain—is at the point of becoming reality. At least there are very advanced experimental prototypes along those lines, and there are already commercially available prostheses with surprising features, which in some cases are superior to human limbs.

Almost Science Fiction

The experimental bionic arm developed by the Rehabilitation Institute of Chicago is one of the most advanced models yet made. It can interpret commands from the brain so that the patient can regain the full functionality of the limb that was lost.

1 The surgeons take the nerves that were connected to the arm and redirect them to muscles of the thorax.

2 When the person fitted with the device wills an action involving the arm, such as raising the arm, the hand, or a finger, the command travels through the nerves, which produce small, precise contractions in the thorax muscles.

3 These contractions are detected by a series of sensors that transmit electrical signals to the computer in the prosthetic arm.

4 The computer then directs the motors to make the arm perform the desired motion.

Half Human, Half Machine

Among the numerous advances forthcoming in the next few years, in addition to bionic arms and legs, are: products stemming from the development of artificial veins, arteries, organs, and muscles; eyes and ears for the blind and deaf; microprocessors that enable quadriplegics to recover the use of their limbs; and even a device to eliminate chronic pain.

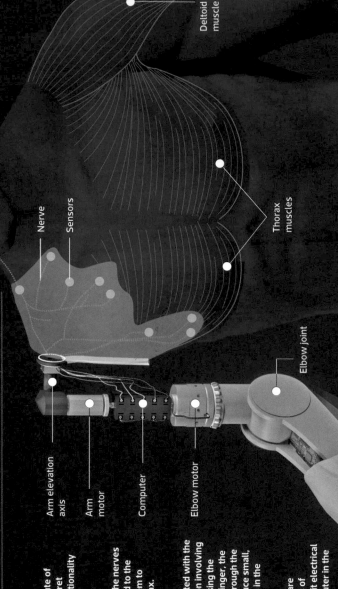

Deltoid muscle

Nerve

Sensors

Thorax muscles

Arm elevation axis

Arm motor

Computer

Elbow motor

Elbow joint

Wrist motor

Flexible wrist

The Intelligent Foot

In contrast to the bionic arm, the Proprio Foot (which was developed by the prosthesis company Ossur and is commercially available) does not interpret commands from the brain. Instead it reproduces the functions of the human foot by taking into account the terrain and the user's movements and gait.

Operation

A device called an accelerometer records the movement of the leg about 1,000 times each second. The computer uses the data to make the appropriate adjustments of the mechanisms in the foot.

Versatility

The Proprio Foot can turn, flex up and down, and carry out adjustments that make walking comfortable, even when going up a slope or climbing stairs—situations that tend to be difficult for amputees.

Automation

In general, it is not necessary for the user to make any adjustments because the prosthesis automatically detects and analyzes changing situations and continually makes its own adjustments.

Always Alert

The Proprio Foot responds, without input from the user, to such situations as being seated in a chair or going up or down stairs.

Sitting

For greater comfort, the prosthesis bends the foot so that its forward tip touches the ground.

On stairs

When the prosthesis detects two stair steps in succession, it rotates the ankle to place the foot in the proper position.

1 billion

The number of persons worldwide who have some type of disability. The figure accounts for 10 percent of the world population.

Robotic Surgery

The use of robots to perform surgeries stopped being a science-fiction fantasy and became a reality about 20 years ago, when the first surgeries of this kind were performed. During unassisted robotic surgery, the surgeon works from a computer console while a robot with special arms operates directly on the patient. This type of surgery enables the surgeon to operate remotely on patients located across the world by using a high-bandwidth connection. Robotic surgery offers numerous advantages, such as extreme precision of the incisions (hand movements are scaled and filtered to eliminate hand tremors) and the small size of incisions, which shortens recovery time for the patient and allows a given doctor to operate on a specific patient without having to be in the same physical location. ●

The Console

is where the surgeon performs the surgical procedure. The virtual-reality environment allows the doctor to observe incisions and organs magnified up to 20 times.

In spite of not operating on a patient directly, the console allows the doctor to "feel" the operation, because the robot transmits data related to flexibility, pressure, and resistance, among other information.

500,000

is the approximate number of robotic surgical procedures that have been performed since the technique was first developed in 1977.

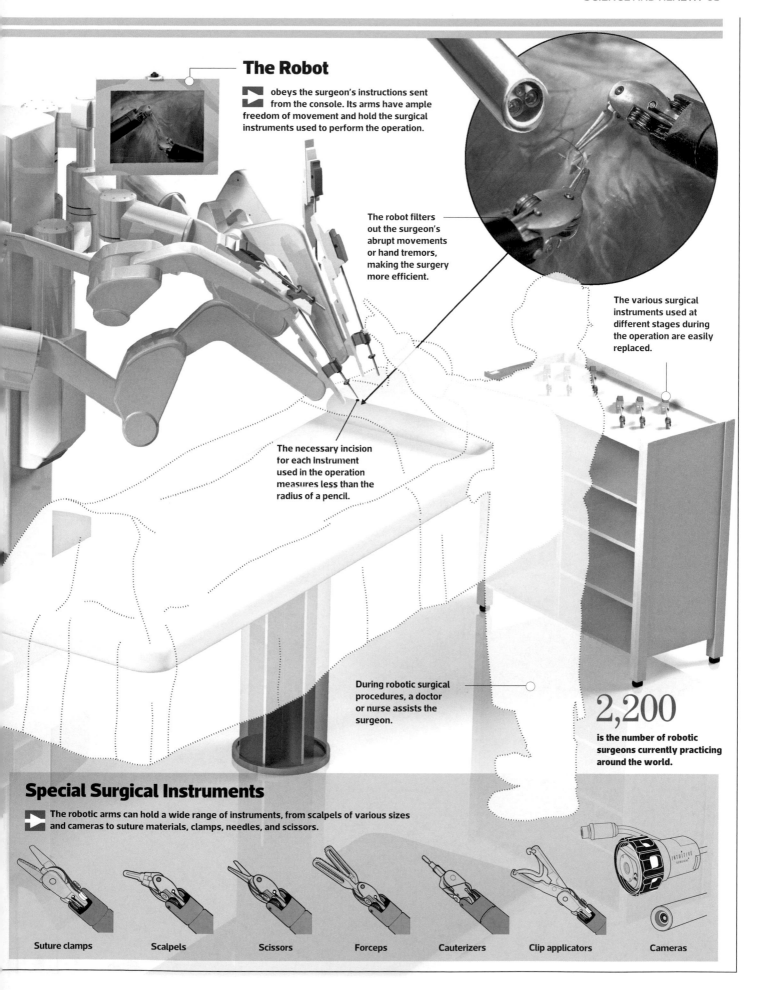

The Robot

obeys the surgeon's instructions sent from the console. Its arms have ample freedom of movement and hold the surgical instruments used to perform the operation.

The robot filters out the surgeon's abrupt movements or hand tremors, making the surgery more efficient.

The various surgical instruments used at different stages during the operation are easily replaced.

The necessary incision for each instrument used in the operation measures less than the radius of a pencil.

During robotic surgical procedures, a doctor or nurse assists the surgeon.

2,200

is the number of robotic surgeons currently practicing around the world.

Special Surgical Instruments

The robotic arms can hold a wide range of instruments, from scalpels of various sizes and cameras to suture materials, clamps, needles, and scissors.

| Suture clamps | Scalpels | Scissors | Forceps | Cauterizers | Clip applicators | Cameras |

Nanobots

One of the most promising aspects of nanotechnology—technology that works on atomic or molecular scales—is the development of nanobots, specialist robots that are thousands of times smaller than the thickness of a human hair. Researchers believe that this type of machine could travel around inside the human body to detect, attack, and destroy malignant cancer cells; repair organs and damaged biological structures; administer specific medications; unblock obstructed arteries; and modify cellular DNA. However, possible applications extend well beyond medical science. For example, among other things, nanobots could prove very useful in cleansing the environment of pollutants.

Nanostructures

The majority of developments in nanotechnology are currently more in the realm of science fiction than everyday reality, although there have been some concrete advances.

Today

NANOTUBES

Tubes formed from a rolled sheet of carbon atoms, which possess surprising properties, such as incredible resistance or the capacity to superconduct at room temperature

FULLERENES

Carbon molecules that are spherical in shape. Their properties are still being investigated, with new applications being discovered every year.

In the Future

DNA
Proposed model of DNA arranged in octahedrons that could form part of the structure of future computers on an atomic scale

NANOMETRIC PUMP
Manufactured from atoms of carbon, oxygen, silicon, hydrogen, and nitrogen

GEARS
Model constructed with carbon nanotubes.

Each little ball represents an atom.

Challenges

 Before the first nanobot can be put to work, researchers must solve a series of basic problems; therefore, it will take some time before this technology can become a reality.

BROWNIAN MOVEMENT

Molecules vibrate violently and uncontrollably because of a physical phenomenon related to the molecular bombardment that a medium exercises over an object within it (as happens, for example, with a grain of pollen in water). On a human scale this movement is imperceptible, but on a nanometric scale, it is sufficiently problematic that nanobot developers need to solve it somehow.

ENERGY

Getting a nanometric object to move through fluid requires considerable energy.

NAVIGATION

How can the path taken by the nanobots be controlled?

COMMUNICATION

How can orders be given to machines as small as molecules? Via chemical stimuli? By means of nanochips? How could they communicate with one another? These are some of the big questions that researchers have yet to answer.

PROPULSION

It is still not clear what the propulsion system should be. However, Swiss and Canadian investigators recently announced the development of a type of "propeller" that imitates the corkscrew movement that bacteria generate with their flagella in order to move, although this technology is still in its infancy.

Comparison

 As of yet, no exact measurement for nanobots has been defined, and this will depend on their capabilities and uses. However, a standard size could be around 50 nanometers—in other words, 140 times smaller than a red blood cell.

7,000 nm

Bacteria
1,000 nm

Prize

The Foresight Nanotech Institute in the United States is offering a prize of $250,000 to the scientist or scientific team that manages to develop a functional nanobot arm measuring less than 100 nanometers, as well as a calculation device that would fit into a space of just 50 cubic nanometers. The prize was announced in 1996, but it has yet to be won.

Conceptual illustration of two nanobots navigating through the inside of a vein

Cutting-Edge Technology

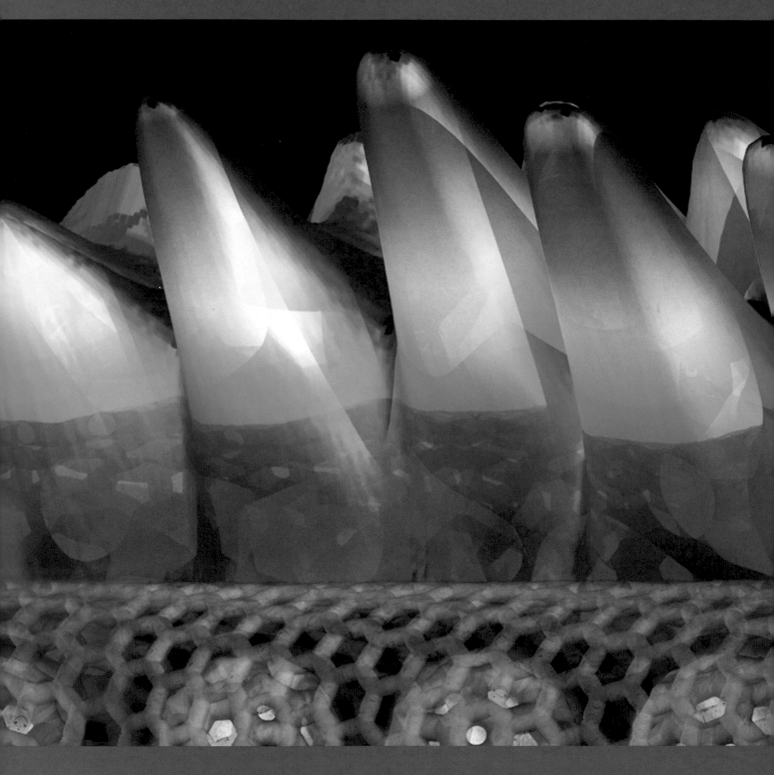

Today, we live with technologies that are already paving the way into the future, and they have started to change our habits. Several recent Japanese documentaries have shown robots being used for educational purposes, to help the teachers with their classes. These types of developments are in their early stages, and there are no doubt many

CARBON NANOTUBES
Carbon nanotubes are among the strongest known fibers. They are composed of one or more graphite sheets or another material and can conduct electricity hundreds of times more efficiently than traditional copper cables.

discoveries and surprises in store. What is certain is that the future has already arrived, and it is unfolding before our eyes. We invite you to discover the numerous applications of nanotechnology and the qualities of intelligent textiles, made with materials that can repel dirt, warm or cool the wearer, release perfumes, or even . . . make the wearer invisible! ●

Smart Houses

The goal of smart-house technology is to develop ways that give a house intelligence so that it can adapt on its own to the needs and wishes of the people who live in it while it also takes care of all the tasks related to home maintenance and security. Even though much of the technology that has been developed for this purpose is too expensive for most people, the continual advances made in this field suggest that in the near future almost all homes will have smart-house devices. ●

Watering the garden
The schedule for watering can be programmed to vary according to the season.

Window blinds
can be programmed to open or close depending on the amount of sunlight.

use photographic images that are downloaded from the Internet and changed periodically.

Occupied-home simulator
When the house is empty for an extended period of time, the system opens blinds and turns on lights and appliances to make it appear that someone is at home.

Light sensors
measure the amount of natural light so that outdoor lighting can be used efficiently.

Primary Functions

SECURITY SURVEILLANCE
■ sounds an alarm when a house intruder is detected.

SECURITY PROTECTION
■ warns of such dangers as fire, water or gas leaks, and electrical faults.

COMFORT AND ECONOMY
■ systems to make the home comfortable and to use energy efficiently.

Emergency lighting

Mail detector

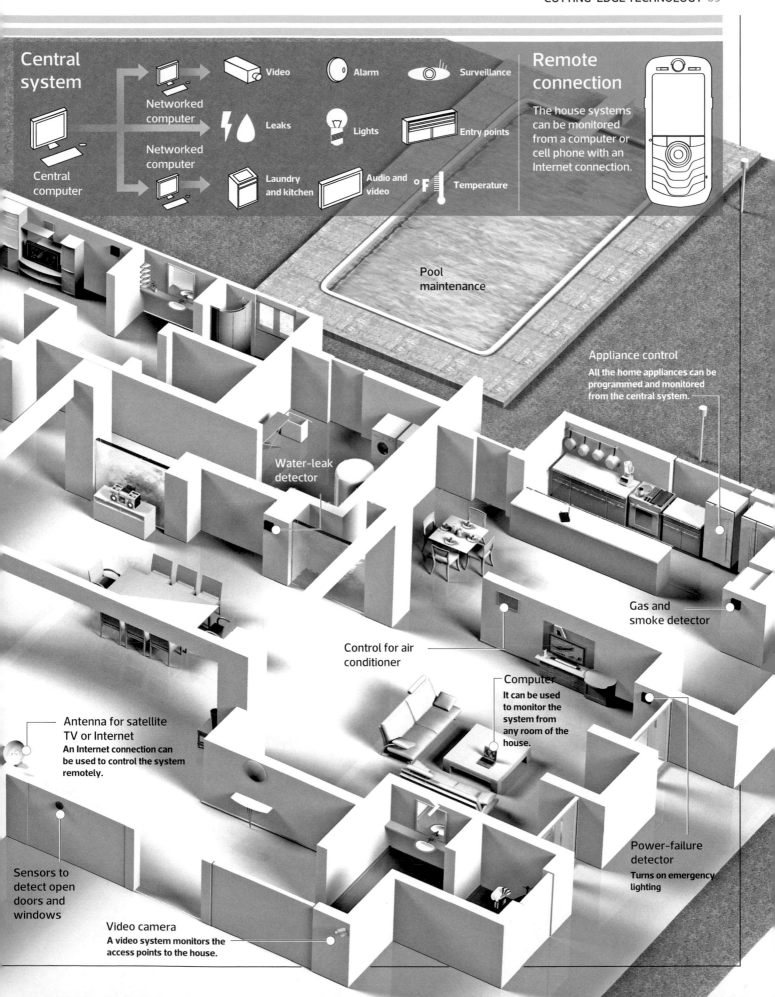

Central system

Central computer

Networked computer

Networked computer

Video

Leaks

Laundry and kitchen

Alarm

Lights

Audio and video

Surveillance

Entry points

°F Temperature

Remote connection

The house systems can be monitored from a computer or cell phone with an Internet connection.

Pool maintenance

Appliance control

All the home appliances can be programmed and monitored from the central system.

Water-leak detector

Gas and smoke detector

Control for air conditioner

Computer
It can be used to monitor the system from any room of the house.

Antenna for satellite TV or Internet
An Internet connection can be used to control the system remotely.

Power-failure detector
Turns on emergency lighting

Sensors to detect open doors and windows

Video camera
A video system monitors the access points to the house.

Nanotechnology

T he term "nanotechnology" refers to the study, design, synthesis, manipulation, and application of materials, devices, and functional systems by controlling matter at the nanoscale. These new, atomically precise structures, such as carbon nanotubes or minuscule instruments to examine the inside of the human body, promise a new technological revolution still difficult to imagine. Specialists in the field expect numerous industrial, scientific, and social breakthroughs. One day, there will be materials that are more resistant than steel yet lighter, cleaner, and more efficient. Among many possible applications that could appear are computers with significantly faster components and molecular sensors capable of detecting and destroying cancer cells in the brain. ●

1 nanometer (nm)

▶ is one-billionth of a meter, or one-millionth of a millimeter (0.04 inch). In other words, it is equivalent to dividing 1 inch into 25 million equal parts.

Challenges

One of the challenges researchers face is how to develop nanotubes of the longest possible length. The longest nanotube to date measures 6 inches (15 cm).

The Crystalline Structure

▶ The structure formed by atoms once they align affects the properties of the material.
One example is pure carbon, which, according to its structure, can become:

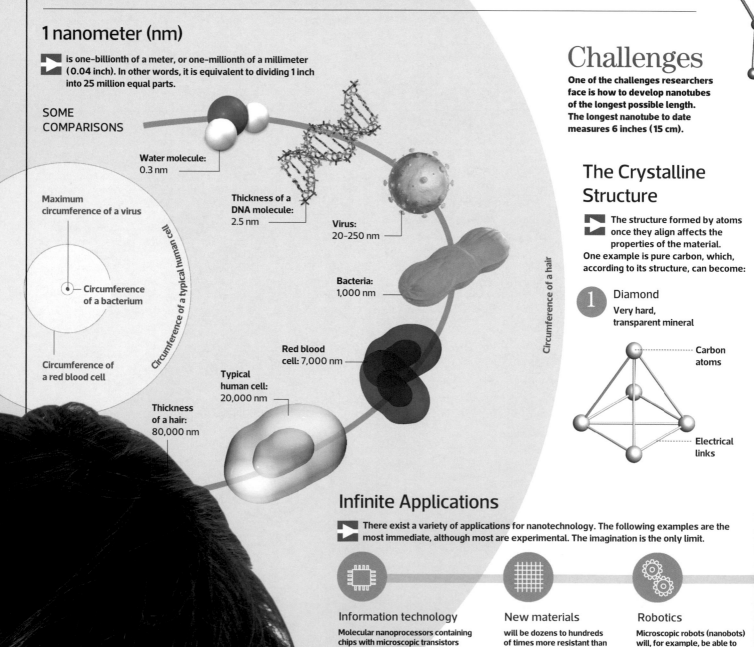

SOME COMPARISONS

Water molecule: 0.3 nm

Thickness of a DNA molecule: 2.5 nm

Virus: 20-250 nm

Bacteria: 1,000 nm

Red blood cell: 7,000 nm

Typical human cell: 20,000 nm

Thickness of a hair: 80,000 nm

Maximum circumference of a virus

Circumference of a bacterium

Circumference of a red blood cell

Circumference of a typical human cell

Circumference of a hair

1 Diamond
Very hard, transparent mineral

Carbon atoms

Electrical links

Infinite Applications

▶ There exist a variety of applications for nanotechnology. The following examples are the most immediate, although most are experimental. The imagination is the only limit.

Information technology

Molecular nanoprocessors containing chips with microscopic transistors will be at the heart of computers millions of times more powerful than those that exist today.

New materials

will be dozens to hundreds of times more resistant than known materials but will also weigh much less.

Robotics

Microscopic robots (nanobots) will, for example, be able to travel inside organs and blood vessels to perform diagnostic tests and repairs.

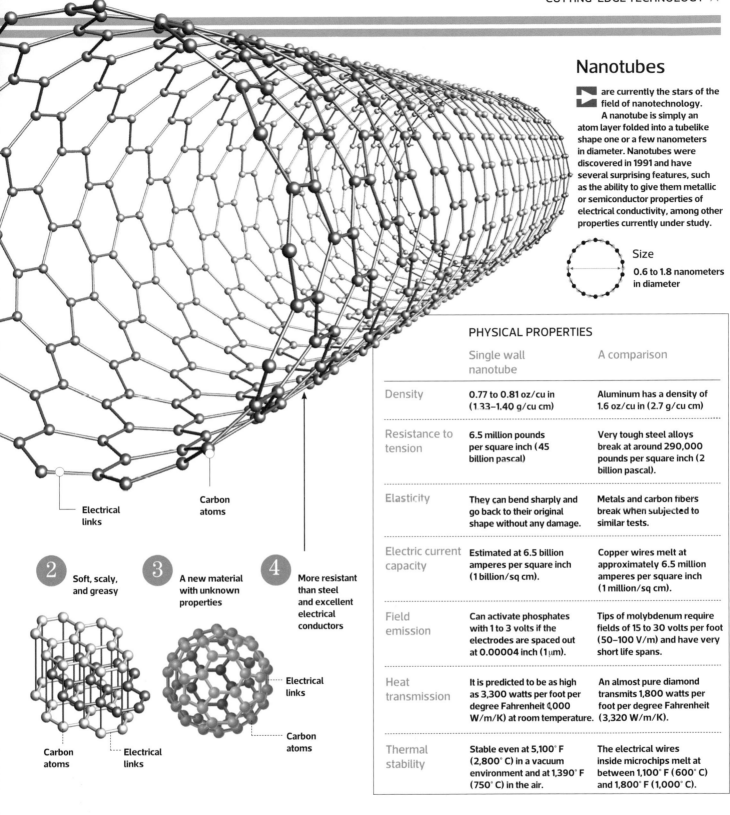

Nanotubes

are currently the stars of the field of nanotechnology. A nanotube is simply an atom layer folded into a tubelike shape one or a few nanometers in diameter. Nanotubes were discovered in 1991 and have several surprising features, such as the ability to give them metallic or semiconductor properties of electrical conductivity, among other properties currently under study.

Size
0.6 to 1.8 nanometers in diameter

Electrical links

Carbon atoms

PHYSICAL PROPERTIES

	Single wall nanotube	A comparison
Density	0.77 to 0.81 oz/cu in (1.33–1.40 g/cu cm)	Aluminum has a density of 1.6 oz/cu in (2.7 g/cu cm)
Resistance to tension	6.5 million pounds per square inch (45 billion pascal)	Very tough steel alloys break at around 290,000 pounds per square inch (2 billion pascal).
Elasticity	They can bend sharply and go back to their original shape without any damage.	Metals and carbon fibers break when subjected to similar tests.
Electric current capacity	Estimated at 6.5 billion amperes per square inch (1 billion/sq cm).	Copper wires melt at approximately 6.5 million amperes per square inch (1 million/sq cm).
Field emission	Can activate phosphates with 1 to 3 volts if the electrodes are spaced out at 0.00004 inch (1 μm).	Tips of molybdenum require fields of 15 to 30 volts per foot (50–100 V/m) and have very short life spans.
Heat transmission	It is predicted to be as high as 3,300 watts per foot per degree Fahrenheit 6,000 W/m/K) at room temperature.	An almost pure diamond transmits 1,800 watts per foot per degree Fahrenheit (3,320 W/m/K).
Thermal stability	Stable even at 5,100° F (2,800° C) in a vacuum environment and at 1,390° F (750° C) in the air.	The electrical wires inside microchips melt at between 1,100° F (600° C) and 1,800° F (1,000° C).

2 Soft, scaly, and greasy

3 A new material with unknown properties

4 More resistant than steel and excellent electrical conductors

Carbon atoms

Electrical links

Electrical links

Carbon atoms

Cosmetics
New smart creams, particularly highly efficient sunblocks

Transmission of electrical energy
Superconducting materials that do not suffer a loss of energy during transportation at room temperature

Medicine
New medicines. Molecular and genetic repairs. Microscopic, protein-building machines, among others.

Clothing
Highly resistant, intelligent fabrics that do not get dirty or that can repel viruses and bacteria

Solar energy
Huge improvements in maximizing this clean and inexhaustible energy source

Data storage
There already exists a memory card that measures just 0.005 square inch (3.2 sq mm) and has a capacity of 100 gigabytes.

Smart Clothing

With the invention of smart fabrics and computerized apparel, our clothing will undergo in the coming years one of the most dramatic and surprising evolutions since humans first began wearing clothes. Some of these new breakthroughs already exist: they are showing up for the first time in the market and are becoming readily available for mass consumption. Among them are materials that integrate features that would have been hard to imagine just a few years ago—for example, clothing that not only informs the wearer of the body's response to physical activity but also modifies itself to improve performance.

Diverse Users

Smart apparel is obviously of great benefit to athletes, but it is also important to patients with chronic illnesses, such as diabetics, who need to monitor their condition frequently.

Sensors

INFORMATION IN REAL TIME

Clothes made out of fabrics with integrated minisensors and imperceptible electrical circuits can determine the wearer's heart rate, blood levels of oxygen and other gases, calories consumed, and breathing rate.

Microphone

Fiber-optic cable

Sensors

Database

Chlorine

is an element found in the fibers of fabrics that repel germs. One of its properties is that it destroys bacterial cell walls. It is also the basis of bleach, which is frequently used in disinfectants.

Smart Fabrics

Generally a product of new developments in nanotechnology, smart fabrics show surprising features that will be widely used in the next few years.

Colorful

A special fiber made of plastic and glass can be used with electronic circuitry that modifies the way the fabric reflects light and thereby changes color.

Comfortable

Fabrics that eliminate sweat, keep the skin dry, and eliminate odors already exist. Similarly, there are materials that can provide ventilation or warmth in accordance with the outside temperature.

Resistant

Fabrics that do not get wrinkled, are resistant to stain, and keep their shape after many years of wear and washing have also been developed.

Antistatic

Fabrics that remove static electricity. They prevent the buildup of hair, pollen, dust, and other potentially harmful particles for people with allergies.

Antimicrobial

Fabrics that block the growth of viruses, fungi, bacteria, and germs.

Transmitter

Perfect Steps

▲ The Adidas-1 shoe, a project three years in the making, can determine the athlete's weight, stride, and surrounding terrain to adjust the shoe's tension accordingly.

1 Inside the hollow heel, the components of the shoe generate a magnetic field.

Magnetic field

2 While running, the foot hits the heel of the shoe and modifies the magnetic field.

Sensor

3 A sensor that can perform up to 1,000 readings per second detects each modification and sends that information to the microchip.

4 A microchip determines the appropriate tension for the heel and sends the information to the motor.

5 The motor, rotating at 6,000 rpm, moves the screw, which in turn strengthens or relaxes the heel. The entire process is repeated with each step.

Heel

Sensor
Motor

Soft heel

Firm heel

5,000,000

is the number of calculations per second performed by the Adidas-1 microchip.

When a person is running, the body absorbs three to four times the person's weight each time a step is taken. Smart shoes help absorb this enormous force and protect the most vulnerable areas, and they also provide comfort and stability.

Biotechnology

The 20th century discovery that all the information that is needed to build a living being is found within each cell, written in a code with only four letters (the DNA molecule), led to the inevitable conclusion that the information could be artificially modified to produce new species with specific qualities or to cure hereditary diseases. Nevertheless, only in recent times have the techniques been developed to attain these objectives. These techniques have yielded products such as transgenic foods that have already become widely available in the marketplace, generating much controversy concerning safety and other issues. ●

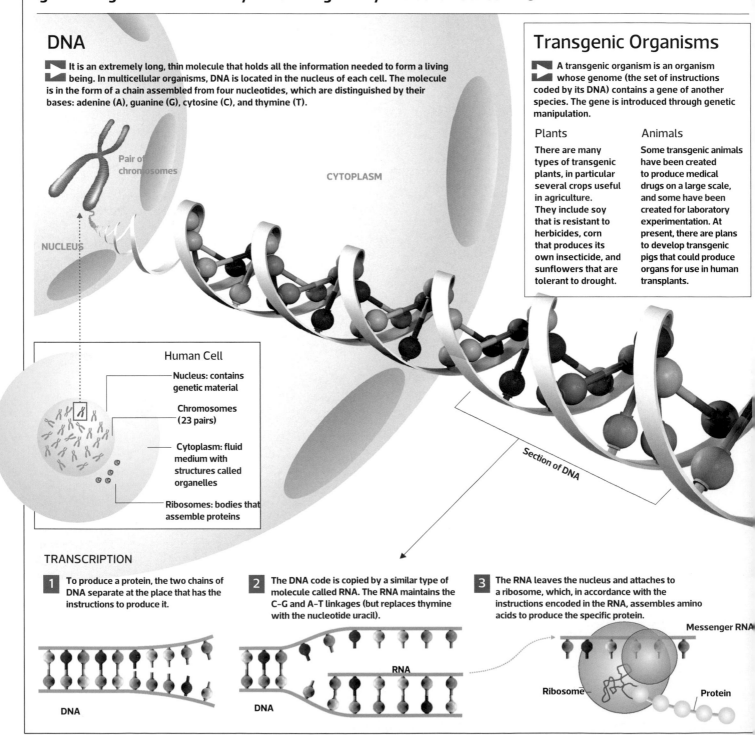

DNA

It is an extremely long, thin molecule that holds all the information needed to form a living being. In multicellular organisms, DNA is located in the nucleus of each cell. The molecule is in the form of a chain assembled from four nucleotides, which are distinguished by their bases: adenine (A), guanine (G), cytosine (C), and thymine (T).

Pair of chromosomes

NUCLEUS

CYTOPLASM

Human Cell

Nucleus: contains genetic material

Chromosomes (23 pairs)

Cytoplasm: fluid medium with structures called organelles

Ribosomes: bodies that assemble proteins

Section of DNA

Transgenic Organisms

A transgenic organism is an organism whose genome (the set of instructions coded by its DNA) contains a gene of another species. The gene is introduced through genetic manipulation.

Plants

There are many types of transgenic plants, in particular several crops useful in agriculture. They include soy that is resistant to herbicides, corn that produces its own insecticide, and sunflowers that are tolerant to drought.

Animals

Some transgenic animals have been created to produce medical drugs on a large scale, and some have been created for laboratory experimentation. At present, there are plans to develop transgenic pigs that could produce organs for use in human transplants.

TRANSCRIPTION

1 To produce a protein, the two chains of DNA separate at the place that has the instructions to produce it.

2 The DNA code is copied by a similar type of molecule called RNA. The RNA maintains the C–G and A–T linkages (but replaces thymine with the nucleotide uracil).

3 The RNA leaves the nucleus and attaches to a ribosome, which, in accordance with the instructions encoded in the RNA, assembles amino acids to produce the specific protein.

DNA

DNA

RNA

Messenger RNA

Ribosome

Protein

Cut and Paste

It is possible to "cut and paste" genes to correct genetic defects or, in the case of transgenic organisms, produce new species with selected properties.

Gene Therapies

Only the first steps have been taken in this specialized field, whose principle is to treat hereditary disorders by modifying a patient's DNA. Other illnesses, such as cancer and AIDS, might also be treatable with this type of therapy.

1 Gene therapy typically makes use of retroviruses to modify a person's DNA. Retroviruses can infect a human cell and use their RNA to modify the cell's DNA to convert the cells into a "virus factory." This capability is used to modify a cell's DNA in a desired way.

2 The retrovirus RNA is modified to reduce or eliminate its ability to cause disease. At the same time, an RNA fragment is added that is intended for insertion into the human cell.

VIRUS

Human Genome

A thorough understanding of the human genome and of the germs that can infect and modify it will make it possible to produce medications that are highly efficient and even tailored to the individual.

NUCLEUS

Chromosome

3 The retrovirus introduces its modified genetic material into the human cell.

The cell functions according to its new instructions.

Ribosome

CYTOPLASM

CELL

3 billion

The approximate number of DNA base pairs that make up the human genome.

Structure

Discovered in 1953, the structure is a double helix whose strands are bridged by bases in an established pattern.

Cytosine — Guanine

Adenine — Thymine

Artificial Intelligence

Although the concept of artificial intelligence (AI) had long been present in science fiction, its theoretical basis was not established until the early 1950s. At first, investigators in the discipline tackled the problem with great optimism, but over the years the challenge of creating a machine that could "feel" and behave like a human being with a capacity for abstraction—and on occasion act in an illogical manner—revealed its considerable complexity. Today there are amazing robots that still lack these human qualities.●

Man's Best Friend

AIBO was one of the most complex robot pets ever created. According to Sony Corp, which introduced the robot in 1999, AIBO interacted with its owner, conveyed emotions by wagging its tail when it was happy, or sought attention when it was being ignored. Manufacturing ceased in 2006, after which more advanced projects began to appear.

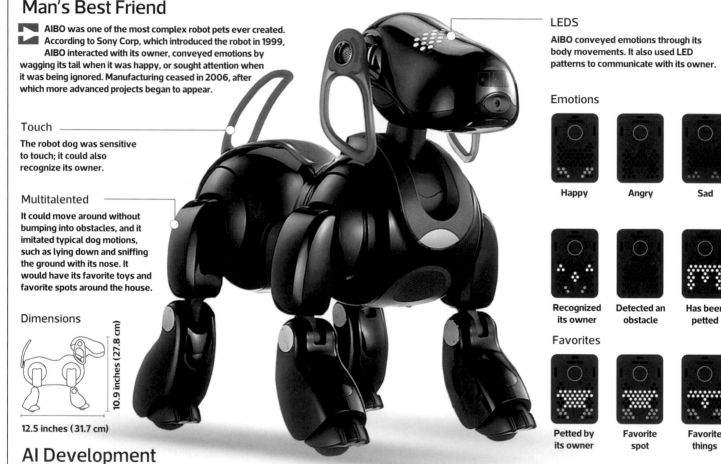

Touch

The robot dog was sensitive to touch; it could also recognize its owner.

Multitalented

It could move around without bumping into obstacles, and it imitated typical dog motions, such as lying down and sniffing the ground with its nose. It would have its favorite toys and favorite spots around the house.

Dimensions

10.9 inches (27.8 cm)

12.5 inches (31.7 cm)

LEDS

AIBO conveyed emotions through its body movements. It also used LED patterns to communicate with its owner.

Emotions

Happy	Angry	Sad

Recognized its owner	Detected an obstacle	Has been petted

Favorites

Petted by its owner	Favorite spot	Favorite things

AI Development

The search for artificial intelligence began in the 1950s. Since then, a number of milestones have been reached. Following are some major milestones.

1950

The Turing test is published. The purpose of the test is to determine whether a machine can be considered intelligent. The challenge consists of having a person converse with a machine and a human being at the same time. If the person cannot decide which interlocutor is the human being, the machine has passed the test. The first machine to pass did so in 2014.

1956

The researcher John McCarthy coins the term "artificial intelligence" at a celebrated Dartmouth Conference.

1962

Unimation, the first company dedicated to producing robots, is formed. Four years later a computer program called ELIZA becomes available. The program uses a dialogue system that simulates a psychotherapist's speech. According to many users/patients, this system can elicit strong emotions from them.

1973

Freddy, a robot capable of identifying and assembling objects, comes into being at the University of Edinburgh, Scotland.

1994

The twin cars VaMP and VITA-2, developed by the University of Munich and Mercedes Benz, drive under automatic control, carrying live passengers about 620 miles (1,000 km) around Paris, in traffic, at speeds up to 80 miles per hour (130 km/h).

1996

The chess program Deep Blue wins a game of chess against world chess champion Garry Kasparov.

The Day a Machine Beat the Best Human

February 10, 1996, is a red-letter day in the history of artificial intelligence. On that day, an IBM computer called Deep Blue won a game of chess in a match against the world chess champion, Garry Kasparov, becoming thereby the first computer to triumph over a reigning world champion. The game was part of a match in which the Russian player prevailed four to two.

In 1997, a rematch was held between Kasparov and Deep Blue, which won by a score of 3.5 to 2.5.

200 million

The possible number of positions evaluated each second by the improved version of Deep Blue that defeated world-chess champion Garry Kasparov.

The robot can run at a speed of 3.7 miles (6 km) per hour and walk at 1.7 miles (2.7 km) an hour.

It has a 52-volt lithium–ion battery mounted in its backpack.

ASIMO

HONDA

Humanoids

Their humanlike appearance could spark our imagination and reinforce the impression that the humanoid is a living machine. At present, commercially sold humanoids serve only as a source of entertainment.

PAPERO

Produced by NEC, PaPeRo is a domestic robot that can recognize the faces of its family members, distinguish colors, read text, dance, and change a TV channel when its owner gives a verbal command. It can tell stories to children, and, by means of its camera eyes, it can send parents images of their children while the parents are at the office.

15.2 inches (38.5 cm)

The robot can lift up to 1 pound (0.5 kg) in each hand.

ASIMO

Honda's bipedal robot ASIMO (Advanced Step in Innovative Mobility) was introduced at the Robodex 2000 exhibition in Yokohama. It can walk, dance, shake hands, carry a tray of drinks like a waiter, and answer simple questions. The current model is about 4 feet 3 inches (1.3 m) tall and weighs 119 pounds (54kg).

1998 1999   2003

Furby, a small pet that resembles a gremlin, is introduced. It can learn to talk as it grows up. It becomes a retail sensation.

Cynthia Breazeal designs Kismet, one of the first robots to respond to people in a natural manner.

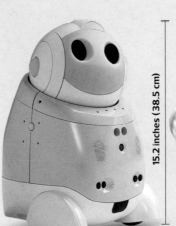

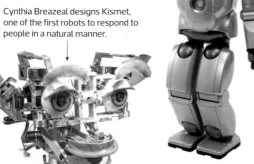

QRIO
A robot made by Sony, QRIO was the first bipedal robot capable of running. It could run at a speed of 45 ft (14 m) per minute.

Virtual Reality

I n full development, the object of virtual reality (VR) is to deceive the senses to create a variety of sensations. It has many applications, many of which are still being explored. The focus has been on forms of entertainment, such as the Oculus Rift headset, in which the player acts within the created setting, and on simulators for training soldiers, pilots, surgeons, and others in extreme situations without placing trainees at risk. Other promising areas for VR—which combines the capabilities of the most powerful computers with ingenious mechanical devices—are in medicine (such as treating phobias and traumas), marketing, and publicity. ●

Images

are created by powerful processors that use various 3-D programming languages. VRML was one of the most widely used, although it gave way to X3-D, which is more complex.

HOW THEY ARE GENERATED

1 The form of the object is generated and given a skeleton framework that, when animated, can be used to modify the shape and position of the object.

2 Textures, colors, and lighting are applied, all of which help provoke sensations of greater realism.

3 The user of the simulation needs to be able to interact with the object by means of the specific characteristics assigned to it.

Requirement

For many years, airline pilots have been required to practice periodically in flight simulators, one of the most widespread applications of virtual reality.

generates 3-D images using complex calculations while it changes perspectives according to the head movements of the person experiencing the simulation.

Uses electromagnetic and inertial sensors to register hand and arm movements, which are converted into electrical signals and incorporated into the simulation.

Deceiving the Senses

SIGHT

There are several means by which high-quality virtual reality misleads the sense of sight. These means include the use of special helmets and glasses and of screens that extend beyond the visual field, such as those employed in IMAX theaters.

SOUND

The challenge is to produce three-dimensional sound that simulates environmental sound. It is necessary to calculate the position of an individual with respect to the virtual sound source and objects. Good-quality simulations exist, but work remains to be done.

SMELL

Virtual-reality simulations have been developed that use strong basic odors, but they are expensive. Producing the sensation of softer and more complex aromas remains a long-term goal.

TOUCH

Some systems use gloves that can give the wearer the perception that virtual objects are present to the touch. However, a good simulation should at the same time include sensations of temperature, shape, firmness, and force—something that remains a distant goal.

TASTE

There have not been advances with this sense. It is believed that to generate taste sensations, it will be necessary to stimulate the brain directly with invasive methods akin to the neuronal sockets envisioned in the movie *Matrix*.

Passage to a Parallel World

▶ Although the perfect virtual-reality setting remains to be created, there are those who already experience new sensations by simply putting on a helmet, a pair of gloves, and special boots.

EARPHONES

are designed to simulate 3-D sound by such techniques as delaying sound output from different channels by a fraction of a second to create the perception that sound sources are situated at distinct locations.

Textures

Researchers recognize that textures are some of the most difficult sensations to simulate. An experimental system that simulates the texture of various grades of sandpaper has been developed in the United States.

Controllers

The most advanced are wireless and detached—that is, unlike a conventional joystick, the controls are not mounted in any kind of structure. They transmit signals to the unit's processor with infrared radiation, and they can register placement, movement, speed, and acceleration through an inertial system.

$739,000,000

was the amount collected worldwide for the movie *Matrix Reloaded* (the final movie of the *Matrix* trilogy), making it one of the top 25 box-office hits of all time. In total, the trilogy would gross $1.7 billion.

BOOTS

function like data gloves by providing information for the simulation. The boots indicate whether the user is running, walking, or resting.

Evolution

▶ In almost half a century of evolution, virtual reality has progressed from an ingenious cinematic machine to a very promising complex technology.

1968
Morton Heilig, a cinematographer, constructs the Sensorama. The viewer sits in a chair that can vibrate. The viewer is surrounded by three screens on which a film, such as a bicycle trip through New York City, is projected. It produces smells, currents of air, and other effects. It was the first virtual-reality simulator.

1968
Ivan Sutherland, a pioneering computer scientist, proposes the use of a video display that can be placed on a viewer's head and respond to the head's orientation to make simulations more real. The result is the head-mounted display (HMD), whose early models use mirrors in a dual-projection system.

The 1980s
1977: The first data glove is patented.

Major development takes place in fighter-aircraft simulators to train pilots using HMD.

1989: The U.S. Department of Defense creates SimNet, a simulation system to train troops.

The 1990s
Many experimental approaches to touch and smell simulators are developed while simulations for vision and sound are perfected.

Perfect Simulation

▶ The *Matrix* trilogy, whose first movie premiered in 1999, presents an idealized virtual reality. It takes place in a world dominated by machines in which human beings live in a fictitious universe. Their brains are connected to a virtual-reality machine that creates such perfect simulations that they cannot even suspect that they inhabit an illusory world.

Soldiers of the Future

For centuries, nations have devised highly diverse means of arming and defending their soldiers. With current developments, the tendency has almost been to think of a soldier as a robotic unit, one that is in constant communication with its fellow soldiers and equipped for combat in any type of terrain, environment, or condition, using weapons that are ever more precise and lethal. Despite these advances, however, the main challenge continues to be that of dealing with the vulnerability of the soldier. Within the most modern uniforms and advanced fighting systems, there is still a human being. In this regard, developments in nanotechnology that could lead to the creation of intelligent uniforms would be truly revolutionary. ●

Land Warrior

is a term used to refer to the most modern and technological approach to equipping a ground soldier. It saw limited use in the Iraq War, but the weight of the equipment and its relatively short battery life led to the suspension of the program. Newer technologies were under study to improve it.

Infrared sensors can detect persons in absolute darkness by the heat they emit.

Camera sight
The image it produces can be viewed directly in the helmet.

Multiple antennas receive and emit signals for radio, GPS, video, and other types of information. The soldier remains in constant contact with other soldiers in the unit, which helps prevent feelings of isolation.

Monocular screen can show the soldier position maps and the placement of troops, among other things. It can also show images from unmanned vehicles.

Control unit
The soldier uses it to control all the systems.

Modular ceramic vest
Divided into plates, it protects the soldier from projectiles the size of an M16 round.

Energy for the system
The system is equipped with lithium batteries and can operate for 24 hours.

Waterproof material maintains normal body temperature, even in extreme conditions.

Mask protects against biological and chemical weapons.

Purification system for food and water provides a constant supply of potable water and of canned or dried rations, with a menu of 24 items.

Boots
Lighter and reduce rubbing

$2 billion

The cost of developing the Land Warrior project over 10 years. Arming each soldier costs less than $30,000.

Unmanned Vehicles

have been designed to provide support, firepower, and reconnaissance without the presence of a human.

COUGAR
Unmanned ground attack vehicle. It provides a high level of firepower without risking the lives of human occupants.

60 hours

is the maximum autonomous flight time of a few types of UAVs, with the record being 81.5 hours. UAVs can perform very abrupt maneuvers that a human crew would not be able to tolerate.

Future Force Warrior

is a planning program for soldiers of the next decade. Various technological systems for defense, vision, and detection will be integrated in the helmet, and the development of nanotechnology could lead to "intelligent" uniforms.

HELMET

integrates infrared vision systems, heat sensors, sensors for chemical and biological weapons, and night-vision cameras. It has a head-up display that the soldier can use to monitor the surrounding area.

Weaponry

Precision bullets that are aimed at a target by detecting body heat

Intimidation

In addition to having lethal systems and weapons, technological soldiers can with their appearance alone produce a psychological impact on the enemy.

Uniform

Lightweight and waterproof, the uniform maintains body temperature and can change color depending on the terrain.

Sensors for detecting toxins. A microchip uses the information to release specific antidotes to protect the soldier.

Biological detectors to monitor such readings as the soldier's blood pressure and pulse

Automatic treatment of wounds by means of intelligent cloth

Masking of body temperature to evade enemy infrared sensors

Gecko technology to help the soldier climb walls

Boot

could be used to store energy from movements by means of kinetic cells.

MULE

A terrestrial vehicle designed for a variety of uses that include transportation, mine detection, and assistance providing air support.

UAV

Unmanned Aerial Vehicles. Small reconnaissance and surveillance aircraft. Some version can carry armament to attack targets.

In the Long Term

Although most of these systems are currently under development, it is unlikely that they will constitute part of regular-issue military equipment before the first 25 years of the 21st century.

- Edible vaccines

- Food with biomarkers that help in identifying troops remotely

- High-nutrition food bars

- Uniforms with protein coating provide shielding from enemy sensors.

- Biometric sensors constantly monitor physiological indicators.

- Clothing to stop bleeding **applies precise pressure on a wounded part of the body.**

- Improved metabolism **can improve the oxygen supply to specific tissues and provide supplementary energy to specific cells.**

- Thermophysiology **Technology for precisely controlling body temperature**

Space Exploration

B y the end of the 20th century, all the planets of the solar system had been visited by space probes, including Uranus and Neptune, the most distant planets. In some cases, the visit was only a flyby mission, which nevertheless provided data impossible to obtain from the Earth. Other missions have involved placing space probes in orbit around a planet. Yet other missions have landed probes on Venus, Mars, and Titan (one of Saturn's moons). In 1969, humans succeeded in walking on the Moon, and there are now plans to send humans to the planet Mars.

Unmanned Spacecraft

All planetary missions have been accomplished with unmanned spacecraft. When possible their voyages have taken advantage of the gravitational field of one or more planets in order to minimize fuel requirements.

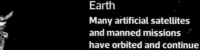

International Space Station

Space Shuttle

The manned spacecraft that has been used the most since its first launching in 1981. The shuttle, however, cannot go beyond a 430-mile (700-km) Earth orbit.

Space Shuttle

Earth

Many artificial satellites and manned missions have orbited and continue to orbit the Earth. The orbiting International Space Station always has a crew onboard.

Moon

The Apollo missions (1969–72) took a total of 12 astronauts to the surface of the Moon. They are the only missions that have taken humans beyond the Earth's orbit. The United States and China are preparing new manned missions to the Moon.

Mercury

Visited in 1974–75 by Mariner 10 on three flybys, with a closest approach of 203 miles (327 km). The probe mapped 45 percent of the planet and made various types of measurements. In 2011, the probe Messenger will enter orbit around Mercury after making flybys in 2008 and 2009.

Venus

The most visited celestial body after the Moon, Venus has been studied by orbiting spacecraft and by landers, many in the 1970s and 1980s. During the Vega and Venera missions and the Mariner and Magellan missions, the surface of the planet was mapped and even excavated, and the atmosphere was analyzed. At present, the spacecraft Venus Express is studying the planet from orbit.

Distance from the Sun	Mercury	Venus	Earth	Mars
36,000,000 miles (57,900,000 km)	67,000,000 miles (108,000,000 km)	93,000,000 miles (150,000,000 km)	141,600,000 miles (227,900,000 km)	

Jupiter

The giant of the solar system was visited for the first time by Pioneer 10 in 1973. Another seven spacecraft (Pioneer 11, Voyagers 1 and 2, Ulysses, Cassini, Galileo, and New Horizons) have made flybys of the planet since then. Galileo studied Jupiter and its moons for eight years from 1995 to 2003, and it transmitted images and data of incalculable scientific value.

Neptune

The distant blue giant has been visited only once, in 1989, by Voyager 2.

Uranus

In 1986, Uranus was visited by Voyager 2, which took photographs and readings of the planet. It is the only mission that has reached Uranus.

7 years

The time it took for the Cassini probe to travel from the Earth as far as Jupiter. Galileo reached Jupiter in six years.

Saturn

Only four missions have visited Saturn. The first three—Pioneer 11 (1979), Voyager 1 (1980), and Voyager 2 (1981)—flew by at distances of 21,000 to 220,000 miles (34,000 to 350,000 km) from the planet. Cassini, in contrast, was placed in orbit around Saturn in 2004, and it has obtained amazing images of the planet and its rings. Part of the Cassini mission was to launch the Huygens probe, which successfully landed on the surface of Saturn's mysterious moon Titan.

Beyond the Solar System

Having left behind the orbit of Neptune, the space probes Pioneer 10 and 11 and Voyager 1 and 2 are bound for the edge of the solar system.

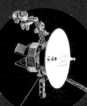

Pioneer 10 and 11

They were launched in 1972 and 1973 and visited Jupiter and Saturn. Contact with the probes was lost in 1997 and 1995, respectively. They carry a plaque with information about the Earth and human beings in anticipation that they may eventually be found by an extraterrestrial civilization. Pioneer 10 is headed toward the star Aldebaran, which it will reach in 1,700,000 years.

Voyager 1 and 2

Launched in 1977, they carry a gold-plated disk with music, greetings in various languages, sounds and photographs from the Earth, and scientific explanations. The probes passed Jupiter, Saturn, Uranus, and Neptune and remain in contact with the Earth. Some data indicate that in 2003 Voyager 1 might have crossed the heliopause, which is at the outer reaches of the solar system.

Eros

In 2000, the probe NEAR entered orbit around the asteroid 433 Eros. In 1986, six spacecraft, among them Giotto, reached Halley's Comet.

Mars

In 1965, Mariner 4 took the first 22 close-up images of Mars. Since then the planet has been visited by many orbiters and by probes that have landed on its surface. Among the most noteworthy are the missions of Viking (1976), Mars Pathfinder (1997), Mars Global Surveyor (1997), and the Mars Exploration Rovers (2004).

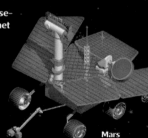

Mars Exploration Rover (2004)

Jupiter
483,000,000 miles
(778,000,000 km)

Saturn
887,000,000 miles
(1,427,000,000 km)

Uranus
1,780,000,000 miles
(2,870,000,000 km)

Neptune
2,800,000,000 miles
(4,500,000,000 km)

Extrasolar Planets

F or centuries, there has been speculation about the possible existence of planets orbiting other stars in the universe in the same way that the planets of the solar system, including the Earth, revolve around the Sun. Nevertheless, it has been only a little more than a decade since it has been possible to detect such bodies—albeit indirectly—thanks to new telescopes and measuring devices with increased sensitivity. The confirmation of the existence of these extrasolar planets suddenly increases the possibility that life might exist in other corners of the cosmos. ●

By late 2007, astronomers had detected more than 225 possible planets in about 200 extrasolar planetary systems. These figures indicate that many of these extrasolar planets form part of a system in which, like the solar system, more than one planet is in orbit around a star.

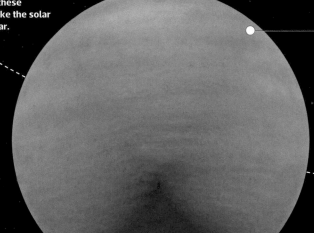

GASEOUS PLANETS

Almost all the extrasolar planets detected to date are gaseous giants like those of the solar system—Jupiter, Saturn, Uranus, and Neptune.

The First Photograph?

In 2004, photographs were taken that might be the first images of stars with extrasolar planets, namely 2M1207b and GQ Lup b (shown in photo). However, it is still under discussion whether these small bodies are true planets or brown dwarfs.

1.2 days

The time it takes the planet OGLE-TR-56 to orbit its star; it is the shortest orbital period known for a planet.

Notable Extrasolar Planets

 Among the extrasolar planets that have been detected, there are surprising differences in their characteristics.

The First	The Hottest	The Most Massive	The Smallest	The Closest	The Most Distant
Pegasi 51 b	HD 149026 b	Undetermined	Gliese 581 c	Epsilon Eridani b	OGLE- 2003 -BLG-235
Discovered in 1995, it was the first extrasolar planet found orbiting a normal star. It is a gaseous planet that has about one-half the mass of Jupiter and lies 47.9 light-years from the Earth.	This gaseous planet is similar to Saturn in terms of mass but smaller in size. It orbits its star at 25th the distance of the Earth from the Sun, and its surface temperature may be more than 2,700° F (1,500° C).	There are several large planetary bodies that are as much as 11 times as massive as Jupiter. Planet-sized objects with a mass above this value are considered to be almost starlike bodies; they are called brown dwarfs and their classi-fication is in question.	Located about 20 light-years from the solar system, it is one of the extrasolar planets thought most likely to resemble the Earth. Its diameter is only 50 percent larger than that of the Earth.	This gaseous Jupiter-sized giant orbits the star Epsilon Eridani, which has characteristics similar to the Sun, although it is somewhat smaller and not as bright. It is only 10.5 light-years from the solar system.	This planet was discovered in 2004 by means of a phenomenon called gravitational microlensing. It is a gaseous giant that revolves around a star at a distance four times greater than that between the Earth and the Sun, and it is about 19,000 light-years away.

STAR

Planetary systems have been found around almost every type of star, including binary and tertiary stars and stars of various sizes and temperatures, a fact that considerably increases the possibility that some planetary systems might be inhabited.

ROCKY PLANETS

With just a few exceptions, the instruments currently used are not able to detect rocky planets like the Earth or Mars. These are the types of planets sought by astronomers, since they are the most likely to be home to life.

12.7 billion years

The age of planet PSR B1620–26b, the oldest of all the known extrasolar planets; this planet orbits a system of binary pulsars. The much-younger Earth is "only" about five billion years old.

A World Similar to the Earth

Of the many extrasolar planets reported by astronomers, Gliese 581 c was the first world discovered to be most like planet Earth. It orbits a red dwarf star, and it is believed to have the basic conditions for the development of life.

EARTH

- **Size:** 7,930 miles (12,756 km) in diameter
- **Mass:** 13.17 x 1024 pounds (5.976 x 465 kg)

- **Distance from its star:** 93 million miles (150 million km), or 1 AU

- **Temperature:** between -112° and 122° F (-80° and 50° C)

- **Orbital period:** 365 days

- **Water:** in gaseous, liquid, and solid states

GLIESE 581 c

- **Size:** 1.5 times the diameter of the Earth
- **Mass:** 4.83 times the Earth's mass

- **Distance from its star:** One 14th the distance of the Earth from the Sun (0.07 AU)

- **Temperature:** unknown, but believed to be between 27° and 104° F (-3° and 40° C)

- **Orbital period:** 13 days

- **Water:** It would have conditions suitable for the existence of liquid water.

Indirect Detection

The extrasolar planets are dark bodies very distant from the solar system, and they always lie in the glare of the star that they orbit.

Therefore, they can generally only be detected by indirect methods, because "seeing" the planet is at present almost impossible.

  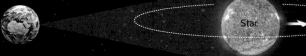 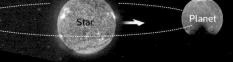  

Star → Planet

SPECTRUM SHOWING REDSHIFT

1 The gravitational force of the planet causes a slight movement of the star toward the planet. The spectrum of the light from the star will show a redshift, which indicates that star is moving away from the Earth.

Planet ← Star

SPECTRUM SHOWING BLUESHIFT

2 When the planet is situated at the opposite side of its orbit, the spectrum of the star will show a blueshift, which indicates that the star is moving toward the Earth.

This process repeats itself over and over, revealing the existence of a planet. For the movement of a planet's star to be noticeable, the planet must exert an appreciable gravitational force, which for the present means that it is only

Tunneling Microscope

M any applications of nanotechnology continue to be explored and developed, but it was the development of the scanning tunnel microscope (STM) that made it possible to see atoms and molecules for the first time. However, this marvelous machine, whose operation is based on the quantum-mechanical concept known as the tunneling effect, is also a powerful tool. Researchers   now continue to use this new tool in the still-advanced technology of manipulating individual atoms and molecules to construct novel materials and structures at a nanometer scale. ●

The Art of Seeing the Small

▶ With the invention of the optical microscope by the early 17th century, it was possible for the first time to overcome the limitations of vision to peer into the world at ever-smaller scales. This invention was followed by the electron microscope, invented around the middle of the 20th century. With the introduction of the scanning tunneling **microscope** in the 1980s, it was finally possible to image individual **atoms**.

HUMAN EYE
▦ **Resolution: one tenth of a millimeter**

OPTICAL MICROSCOPE

Uses visible light focused by lenses. The microscope's resolution is limited by the size of the wavelengths of light.

● **Magnification** up to 2,000 times	▦ **Resolution:** 200 nanometers	◉ **Images:** transparent, two dimensional

TRANSMISSION ELECTRON MICROSCOPE

It illuminates the sample with focused beams of electrons—that is, it uses shorter wavelengths than those of visible light and thereby overcomes light's limitation.

● **Magnification** up to 1,000,000 times	▦ **Resolution:** 0.5 nanometers	◉ **Images:** transparent, two dimensional

SCANNING ELECTRON MICROSCOPE

scans the sample with a beam of electrons and reads the surface.

● **Magnification of** up to 1,000,000 times	▦ **Resolution:** 10 nanometers	◉ **Images:** opaque, three dimensional

SCANNING TUNNELING MICROSCOPE

Based on quantum principles, it makes atomic-scale imaging possible.

● **Magnification** of up to 1,000,000,000 times	▦ **Resolution:** 0.001 nanometer (vertical) and 0.1 nanometer (horizontal)	◉ **Images:** three-dimensional graphical images of atomic structures

THE TUNNELING CURRENT

is a current of electrons that pass between the sample and probe by means of the tunneling effect. The current is generated by applying a voltage between the sample and the probe. The intensity of the current varies according to the distance between the tip of the probe and the sample—in other words, according to the relief of the sample.

Nobel Prize

The physicists Gerd Binnig (German) and Heinrich Rohrer (Swiss) in 1981 established the theoretical groundwork for the development of the STM. For this work they were awarded the Nobel Prize for Physics in 1986.

THE STM PROBE

The tip of the probe is an electrical conductor that is free of oxides and comes to as sharp a point as possible—ideally a single atom.

THE SAMPLE

for an STM must be either metallic or a semiconductor, and it must be very smooth. Its surface roughness should be less than one thousandth of a millimeter.

The STM in Action

To see atoms the STM reads the surface of an object with an extremely fine point, comparable to the way a person can use the tip of a finger to read Braille by detecting patterns of raised dots.

The process for reading the surface at an atomic scale requires producing a tunneling current between the STM probe and the sample. For this reason, the entire microscope functions like an electrical circuit.

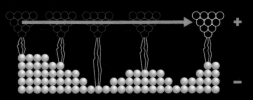

The Result

is a graphic that shows the peaks and valleys of the sample's atomic and electronic structure.

The processor converts the variations in tunneling-current intensity registered by the probe into graphics that represent the atomic structure at the surface of the sample.

The Tunneling Effect

is quantum-mechanical in nature. There is nothing analogous on the scale of humans and everyday objects.

IN CLASSICAL PHYSICS

a particle cannot pass through an energy barrier (a potential barrier) if the energy of the barrier is greater than that of the particle.

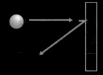

IN QUANTUM MECHANICS

a particle does not have a concrete location. Instead, the particle has wavelike properties and its position is defined in terms of a probability cloud, which extends beyond the barrier. In this way, the particle can cross the barrier by, in effect, tunneling through it.

The wave is reflected by the wall

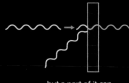

but a part of it can pass through.

Thanks to the tunneling effect, electrons pass from the STM probe to the sample despite the barrier presented by the vacuum between them. The strength of this tunneling current is measured to determine the placement of the atoms on the sample being studied.

Manipulation of Atoms

One of the most astonishing applications of STM is the manipulation of individual atoms and molecules as building blocks in microscopic constructions. This experimental technology might lead to the creation of new materials with unsuspected properties.

1 The probe is first used in its scanning mode to identify the atom to be moved.

2 The tip approaches the atom until it almost touches. The attractive forces generated by the tip of the probe can then pull the atom along the surface of the sample.

3 The strength of the probe's electrical field is reduced to release the atom into the desired position.

Hadron Collider

The Large Hadron Collider (LHC) is a very large scientific instrument at the European Organization for Nuclear Research (CERN). It is installed in an underground tunnel that is in the form of a ring about 5.3 miles (8.5 km) in diameter and underlies the border between France and Switzerland. The function of the instrument is to make particles collide with great energy to break them apart and obtain data concerning the basic forces of the universe. This information can lead to the discovery of new elementary particles as well as confirm the presence of elementary particles whose existence has only been determined theoretically. ●

SWITZERLAND

Lake Geneva

FRANCE

Geneva

0 miles 10

The rings
The tunnels are circular, and their depth below the surface ranges from 330 to 574 feet (100 to 175 m).

Collision of particles

7.9 feet (2.9 m)

150 feet (45.7 m)

ATLAS DETECTOR

An instrument designed to explore, through particle collisions, the fundamental nature of matter and the basic forces that govern the universe. It weighs 7,700 tons (7,000,000 kg).

The Complex

▲ is made up of a number of tunnels in the form of rings, each of which raises the energy of the particles for the next ring. Superconducting magnets accelerate and guide the particles. Six experiments analyze the results of the collisions.

— Hydrogen ions (single protons) or lead ions

ALICE

ATLAS

1.40 mile (2.25 km)

SPS

LHCb

5.30 miles (8.53 km)

PS

1 A linear particle accelerator separates atom nuclei from their electrons to form ions. Some ions contain just one proton (hydrogen ions), but others have more than one (such as lead ions). These ions are directed to the underground complex.

2 The ions are accelerated to reach speeds close to that of light.

3 Powerful impulses of radio waves raise the energy of the ions to 400 billion electron volts.

Big Bang

The Large Hadron Collider, by obtaining data concerning elementary particles and fundamental forces, will make it possible for us to learn the properties of the universe a fraction of a second following the big bang, the great initial explosion of the universe.

A Record of the Collision

The particles that collide at high energy produce many elementary particles that exist for only millionths of a second, and they must be detected and analyzed in that short amount of time.

CMS

— Muon
— Electron
— Photon
— Charged hadron
···· Neutral hadron

Electromagnetic calorimeter
Hadron calorimeter
Superconductor magnet
Collision of particles
Muon detector
Silicon tracker
Entry of the particles that will collide.

Large Hadron Collider

In the LHC, either high-energy protons or high-energy lead ions collide against each other. Upon breaking apart as a result of the collisions, fundamental particles are generated in millionths of a second.

17 miles (27 km)

Streams of billions of now very highly energized ions are introduced into the LHC accelerator, some in one direction and others in the opposite direction. Superconducting magnets then increase their energy tenfold before particles are made to collide with each other.

CMS Detector

This instrument, which weighs 13,800 tons (12,500,000 kg), is designed to analyze the particles (such as photons, muons, and other fundamental particles) that are generated between protons at extremely high energies and to determine their mass, energy, and speed.

Superconducting magnets Cooled to almost absolute zero (about −459° F, or −273° C) with liquid nitrogen, the magnets are the largest that have ever been built. They impart high energy to the particles and guide them.

Muon detector permits the detection of this fundamental particle and allows for the measurement of its mass and velocity.

49 feet (15 m)
70.5 feet (21.5 m)

Silicon tracker It tracks charged particles and measures their speed and mass.

Electromagnetic calorimeter precisely measures the energy of lightweight elementary particles, such as electrons and photons.

Hadronic calorimeter records the energy of the hadrons and analyzes their interaction with atomic nuclei.

Entry of the particles that will collide.

4

Glossary

Alphanumeric

Formed of letters, numbers, and other characters.

AM

In telecommunications, amplitude modulation (AM) is the linear modulation of the information-carrying wave. It consists of varying the amplitude of the wave in accordance with variations in the level of information being transmitted.

Amino Acid

Type of molecule that contains a free carboxyl group (-COOH) and a free amine group (-NH2). Amino acids are generally represented by the formula NH2-CHR-COOH, where R is a radical or side chain characteristic of each amino acid. Many of the amino acids form proteins.

Amplitude

In wave mechanics, the amplitude of a wave is the maximum value, both positive and negative, of the wave. The maximum positive value is called the "peak or crest" and the maximum negative value the "trough or valley."

Atomic Number

A positive whole number that is equal to the total number of protons in an atomic nucleus. It is usually represented by the letter Z. It is a characteristic of each chemical element and represents a basic property of the atom: its nuclear charge.

Barcode

Barcodes are codes based on a set of vertical parallel lines of varying thickness and spacing that, taken as a whole, represent specific information. Barcodes enable the swift identification of goods at a particular point in the logistical chain, thereby facilitating their tracking through a distribution network from manufacturer or supplier to consumer, with real-time information concerning inventory levels enabling automated scheduling of shipments. These days the use of barcodes is extremely widespread on a global basis.

Catalyst

A substance capable of accelerating or retarding a chemical reaction, while itself remaining unaltered (it is not consumed during the reaction). This process is called catalysis. Catalysts do not alter the final energy balance of the chemical reaction but simply allow equilibrium to be attained at a greater or lesser speed.

Catheter

In medicine this is a tube that may be inserted into tissue or a vein. Catheters allow the injection of drugs, the drainage of fluids, and also the insertion of other medical instruments.

Cell

This is the principal structural and functional unit of living beings. Its name comes from the Latin *cellulae* and means "small compartment" or cell.

CFC

Abbreviation of chlorofluorocarbon, a name that refers to each of the derivatives of saturated hydrocarbons obtained by substituting hydrogen atoms with chlorine and fluorine atoms. Their high degree of physicochemical stability means they have been widely used as refrigerating liquids, extinguishing agents, and aerosol propellants.

Chromosome

Each of the elongated bodies of a cell nucleus containing genetic material is called a chromosome. Each chromosome is made up of a macromolecule of DNA associated with proteins. There is a constant number of chromosomes for any given species—in human beings it is 46.

Convection

Convection is one of the three forms of heat transfer and is characterized by the displacement of matter between regions of different temperature. Convection only takes place in fluids (including air). When fluids are heated, their density decreases and they rise, being displaced by those parts at a lower temperature that, in turn, descend and are heated to repeat the cycle.

CPU

Abbreviation for central processing unit. This component executes program instructions and controls the functions of the different components of a computer. It is usually incorporated into a chip known as a microprocessor.

Diffraction

In physics, diffraction refers to a phenomenon associated with wave propagation, such as the spreading and bending of waves when they meet an obstacle. Diffraction occurs with all types of waves, whether they are sound waves, waves on the surface of a fluid, or electromagnetic waves such as light and radio waves. In the electromagnetic spectrum, the lengths of X-ray waves are similar to the interatomic distances within matter. Therefore, the diffraction of X-ray waves is used as a method to explore the nature of crystalline structures. This technique allowed for the discovery of the double helix structure of DNA in 1953.

Diode

A device that allows electric currents to pass in a single direction. Below a given difference of potential, it behaves like an open circuit (that is, it does not conduct), and above it, the diode acts as a closed circuit with very low electric resistance. As a result of this behavior, diodes are usually known as rectifiers because they can convert alternating current to direct current.

DNA

Abbreviation of deoxyribonucleic acid. This is the primary chemical component of chromosomes and the material of which genes are formed. Its function is to provide a blueprint for the manufacture of a living being identical to the one from which it comes (or, very similar, in the event that it is mixed with another chain, such as is the case with sexual reproduction).

Electric Circuit

An electric circuit is a series of electric elements or components, such as resistors, condensers, and power supplies, electrically connected to each other with the aim of generating, carrying, or modifying electronic signals.

Electromagnetic Radiation

Combination of electric and magnetic fields oscillating perpendicularly to each other, which is propagated through space and transports energy from one place to another. Unlike other types of waves, which require a material medium to propagate, electromagnetic radiation can propagate in a vacuum.

Enzyme

An enzyme is a biomolecule that can catalyze a chemical reaction. The name comes from the Greek word énsymo, meaning "in yeast." Enzymes are proteins. Some RNA fragments are also able to catalyze reactions related to the replication and maturation of nucleic acids.

EVA

EVA (ethylene vinyl acetate), also known as foam rubber, is a thermoplastic polymer that offers good resistance to the weather and chemicals, has low water absorbency, is environmentally friendly, and can be thrown away, recycled, or incinerated. Applications include school supplies, footwear, set design, and handicrafts. It is washable and nontoxic.

FM

In telecommunications, frequency modulation (FM) is the process of codifying information, in both digital and analog form, in a carrier wave by means of the instantaneous variation of its frequency in accordance with the input signal.

Frequency

In wave mechanics, frequency is defined as the number of oscillations (or complete cycles) of a wave per unit of time (generally per second). Humans are able to hear frequencies between 20 and 20,000 hertz (cycles per second).

Gene

The basic unit of inheritance in living beings. In molecular terms, a gene is a linear sequence of nucleotides in the DNA molecule containing all the information necessary to synthesize a macromolecule with a specific cellular function. Genes are found along each of the chromosomes, occupying a specific position called a locus. A species' particular set of chromosomes is known as a genome.

GPS

The abbreviation for Global Positioning System—a system that makes it possible to establish the position of a person, car, or ship anywhere in the world. The GPS operates by means of a network of orbiting satellites with trajectories that have been synchronized to cover the entire surface of the Earth.

Hadron

In physics, a hadron is a subatomic particle that experiences strong interaction with the nucleus.

Hardware

This term covers all the material components of a computer. These include the electronic and electromechanical devices as well as circuits, cables, cards, cases, peripherals, and other physical elements related to the computer.

Hertz

Unit of frequency forming part of the International System of Units. It is named after the German physicist Heinrich Hertz, who discovered the transmission of electromagnetic waves. Its symbol is Hz. A hertz represents a cycle per second, where a cycle is understood to be the repetition of an event.

Humanoids

Autonomous robots of a similar appearance, height, and weight to humans. They can see, hear, and learn the majority of human activities.

Land Warrior

Military gear that looks very similar to that worn in the film The Terminator (1984) starring Arnold Schwarzenegger. The wearable system includes electronic weapons, body-mounted computers, and a range of systems that protect against chemical attacks.

Liquid Crystal

A device invented by Jack Janning. This is an electric system for displaying data. It consists of two transparent conductive layers that sandwich a special crystalline material (liquid crystal) with the capacity to rotate light as it passes through. A liquid crystal display's (LCD) basic material is liquid crystal, which exhibits behavior similar to that of liquids. LCD screens are found in a multitude of industrial and consumer goods: cash machines, household appliances, telecommunications equipment, computers, etc.

Logarithm

In mathematics, a logarithm of a given number to a given base is the power to which the base must be raised to get the number. For example, the logarithm of 1,000 to the common base 10 is 3, because 10 raised to a power of 3 is 1,000 (that is, 10 times 10 times 10 is 1,000).

Macromolecule

Molecules with a high molecular weight, composed of a large number of atoms. Macromolecules are generally the result of the repetition of one or a small number of minimal units (monomers) that make up polymers. They can be organic or inorganic, and many of them are very important to the field of bio-chemistry. Plastics are a type of synthetic organic molecule.

Microprocessor

An assembly of highly integrated electronic circuits that are used in computer calculation and control. In a computer, it is the central processing unit (CPU).

Modulation

This is the name given to the set of telecommunications techniques that make it possible to transport information on a carrier wave. These techniques permit better use of a communication channel, making it possible to transmit more information simultaneously and protecting it from possible interference and noise.

Monomer

A molecule of low molecular weight that can link to other monomers by means of chemical bonds to form polymers. The word "monomer" comes from the Greek *mono* ("one") and *mero* ("part").

Nanobots

Special robots that are thousands of times smaller than the thickness of a human hair.

Nanotechnology

The development and production of tiny devices, with sizes less than 100 nanometers (1 nanometer [nm] is equal to 10^{-9} meters). It is hoped that in the future nanotechnology will make it possible to obtain materials with extremely precise compositions and properties. These materials may provide structures with an unprecedented level of strength and may allow for the development of extraordinarily compact and powerful computers. Nanotechnology may lead to revolutionary methods of atom-by-atom production and may make the practice of surgery possible on a cellular scale.

OCR

Abbreviation for optical character recognition. This software detects the characters in an im-age that make up a text and stores them in a format compatible with word-processing programs. In addition to the text itself, it can also detect the format and language used.

PAL

Phase alternating line (PAL) is a coding system used in the transmission of analog color television signals across most of the world. Developed in Germany, it is used in the majority of African, Asian, and European countries, as well as in Australia and some Latin American countries.

Photoelectric Cell

A photoelectric cell, also called a photovoltaic cell, is a light-sensitive electric device that is capable of producing electricity. A group of photoelectric cells is called a photovoltaic panel, a device that converts solar radiation into electricity.

Polymer

In general, an organic macromolecule formed from the union of molecules and monomers. The term is derived from the Greek word *polys*, meaning "many," and *meros*, meaning "parts."

Praxinoscope

An optical device invented in 1877 by Charles-Émile Reynaud. It used a series of images drawn on strips of paper placed in spinning cylinders. A system of mirrors allowed the spectator, who looked into the cylinders from above, to enjoy the illusion of movement. In 1889 Reynaud developed the Théâtre Optique, an improved version that projected the images drawn on longer strips of paper onto a screen. The appearance of the Lumière brothers' projector eclipsed this precursor of animated cartoons.

Propellant

This is the gas used to displace the substances contained in aerosols. CFCs were the most widely used until their effect of weakening the ozone layer was discovered. Another propellant used in aerosols is butane.

Prostaglandin

Any member of a group of substances derived from fatty acids containing 20 carbon atoms. They are considered cellular mediators with a variety of effects that are frequently in opposition to one another. The name "prostaglandin" derives from the prostate gland. When prostaglandins were isolated for the first time in seminal fluid in 1936, it was believed that they formed part of the secretions from the prostate. In 1971 it was discovered that acetylsalicylic acid and its derivatives can inhibit the synthesis of prostaglandins.

Recycling

The process of reusing parts or elements of an object, technology, or device that can still be used, even though they belong to something that has already reached the end of its useful life.

Semiconductor

A substance that acts as a conductor or insulator depending on the electric field in which it is placed. The most common semiconductor element is silicon. Other semiconductors are germanium, selenium, tellurium, lead, antimony, sulfur, and arsenic.

SMS

Abbreviation for short message service. SMS makes it possible to send short messages be-tween cellular phones, fixed phones, and other handheld devices. SMS was designed originally as part of the GSM (global system for mobile communications) standard, but it is now available on a wide variety of networks.

Software

All the programs and routines required to carry out a specific task on a computer. The name is used to distinguish it from hardware, a system's physical components.

Specific Weight

This is the weight per unit volume of a material. Under the decimal metric system it is measured in kilograms-force per cubic meter (kgf/m^3). Under the International System of Units, it is measured in newtons per cubic meter (N/m^3).

Stroboscope

An instrument used to make a cyclically moving object appear to be stationary or slow moving. It makes it possible to turn light on and off at given intervals and as often as is required. This device was used on record-player turntables as an indicator that the turntable was rotating at the right speed.

Telecommunications

This refers to the technology allowing a mes-sage to be transmitted from one place to an-other, normally with the additional typical attribute of being bidirectional. It comes from the Greek *tele*, meaning "distance." This term covers all forms of communication over distance (radio, telegraph, television, telephone, data transmission, and computer networks).

Textile Microcapsules

These are tiny containers inside the structure of cloth that allow it to benefit from substances that are sometimes in a liquid state. An example is thermal cloth with microcapsules of paraffin: if the temperature varies, the paraffin changes state from solid to liquid (or vice versa) and thus maintains a constant temperature.

Thermodynamics

The branch of physics that studies energy and how it is transformed into its various states such as heat, as well as its capacity to carry out work. It is intimately related to statistical mechanics from which numerous thermodynamic relations can be derived. Thermodynamics studies physical systems at a macroscopic level, whereas statistical mechanics usually provides a microscopic description of them.

Toner

Also known as "dry ink" because of its functional analogy with ink. It is a fine dust, normally black in color, that is deposited by electrostatic attraction on the paper being printed. Once it has adhered, the pigment is fixed to the paper by appropriate levels of pressure or heat. Because no solvents are involved, the process was originally known as xerography, from the Greek *xeros*, meaning "dry."

Transgenic

This is the name given to genetically modified organisms, specifically those whose genetic material has been deliberately designed or altered. The first transgenic organisms date back to the 1950s when strains of commercial yeast were modified by irradiation. The genetic modification of organisms is an extremely controversial subject; ecological organizations say that the risks of transgenic organisms have not yet been fully determined and warn that they could spread out of control, "contaminating" natural crops. On the other hand, defenders of transgenics argue that this type of technology could be used to mitigate world hunger and to reduce the impact of a range of illnesses (for example, it is possible to produce rice that is significantly richer in certain nutrients, preventing deficiency diseases, or cows that could yield milk containing vaccines or antibiotics).

Transistor

An electronic semiconductor device used to amplify electric currents, generate electric oscillations, and carry out functions such as modulation, detection, and switching.

Trigonometry

Trigonometry (which in Greek means "the measurement of triangles") is a branch of mathematics that studies angles, triangles, and the relationships between them (trigonometric functions). It has many applications. For example, triangulation techniques are used in astronomy to measure distances to the nearer stars and in geography to measure distances between geographic points; it is also used in satellite navigation systems.

Tungsten

Also called wolfram, tungsten is a chemical element that has the symbol W and atomic number 74. A very hard, heavy, steel-gray to white transition metal, tungsten is found in several ores including wolframite and scheelite and is remarkable for its robust physical properties, especially the fact that it has the highest melting point of all the non-alloyed metals and the second of all the elements after carbon. It is used in incandescent lightbulb filaments, in electric resistors, and, alloyed with steel, in the manufacture of tools.

Virtual Reality

Simulations created by a computer to achieve a certain end. Virtual reality is considered in many ways to be the definitive interface be-tween humans and computers. It basically consists of simulating all a person's possible perceptions, such as graphics for sight, sound, touch, and even the feeling of acceleration or movement. All these different sensations must be presented to users in a way that they feel immersed in the universe generated by the computer, to the point where they cease to perceive reality and are deceived into imagining that they have been transported to the other side of the screen, as if to a new world.

Wavelength

In wave mechanics, this is the name given to the distance between two points, measured in the direction of propagation of a wave, at which the state of movement is identical, such as between adjacent peaks or troughs.

Wiimote

This is the primary control for a Nintendo Wii console. Its most outstanding features are its ability to detect movement in space and its skill in pointing at objects on the screen.

For More Information

Museum of the Moving Image

36-01 35th Avenue
Queens, NY 11106
(718) 777-6800
Website: http://www.movingimage.us
This museum for all ages hosts screenings, public discussions, educational programs, and interactive tours on the technology behind film, television, and other digital media throughout history to modern day.

New York Hall of Science

47-01 111th Street
Corona, NY 11368
(718) 699-0005
Website: http://nysci.org/visit_main/contact
Originally built as an attraction in the 1964 World's Fair, the hall features more than 450 interactive exhibits in both an indoor and an outdoor space with installments such as Rocket Park and the Science Playground tailored to educating young aspiring scientists.

National Video Game Museum

8004 North Dallas Parkway
Frisco, Texas 75034
(972) 668-8400
Website: http://www.nvmusa.org
Opened in 2016, this museum offers a detailed view into the history, production, and future of video games.

The International Society for Technology in Education

1530 Wilson Boulevard, Suite 730
Arlington, VA 22209
(703) 348-4784
Website: https://www.iste.org
This non-profit organization allows students and teachers to connect with developing technology and educational standards.

Rehabilitation Engineering and Assistive Technology Society of North America (RESNA)

1560 Wilson Bvd
Suite 850
Arlington, VA 22209

(703) 524-6686

Website: http://www.resna.org

This organization helps people with disabilities and educational institutions understand and connect with advancing technology.

Association of Science – Technology Centers

818 Connecticut Avenue NW
7th Floor
Washington, DC 20006-2734
(202) 783-7200
Website: www.astc.org

Through strategic alliances and global partnerships, the Association of Science-Technology Centers (ASTC) strives to increase awareness of the valuable contributions its members make to their communities and the field of informal STEM learning.

WEBSITES

Because of the changing nature of internet links, Rosen Publishing has developed an online list of websites related to the subject of this book. This site is updated regularly. Please use this link to access the list:

http://www.rosenlinks.com/VES/tech

For Further Reading

Aspray, William, Campbell-Kelly, Martin, Ensmenger, Nathan, and Jeffrey R. Yost. *Computer: A History of the Information Machine.* Boulder, CO. Westview Press, 2014.

Foran, Racquel. *Robotics: From the Automatons to the Roomba.* History of Science. Essential Library, 2015.

Isaacson, Walter. *The Innovators: How a Group of Hackers, Geniuses and Geeks Created the Digital Revolution.* New York, NY: Simon and Schuster Paperbacks, 2015

Isabella, Orlando, Jager, Klaus, Smets, Arno, Van Swaaij, Rene, and Miro Zeman. *Solar Energy: The Physics and Engineering of Photovoltaic Conversion, Technologies and Systems.* Cambridge, England. UIT Cambridge Ltd., 2016

Kahney, Leander. *Jony Ive: The Genius Behind Apple's Greatest Products.* New York, NY. The Penguin Group, 2013.

Kelly, Kevin. *The Inevitable: Understanding the 12 Technological Forces That Will Shape Our Future.* New York, NY: Viking, 2016.

Milner, Greg. *How GPS is Changing Technology, Culture, and Our Minds.* New York, NY: W.W. Norton & Company, Inc., 2016.

Pyle, Rod. *Amazing Stories of the Space Age: True Tales of Nazis in Orbit, Soldiers on the Moon, Orphaned Martian Robots, and Other Fascinating Accounts from the Annals of Spaceflight.* Amherst, NY. Prometheus Books, 2017.

Thompson, Clive. *Smarter Than You Think: How Technology Is Changing Our Minds for the Better.* New York, NY. Penguin Group, 2013.

Wootton, David. *The Invention of Science: A New History of the Scientific Revolution.* New York, NY: HarperCollins Publishers, 2015.

Index